Dreams on Film

Dreams on Film

The Cinematic Struggle Between Art and Science

by Leslie Halpern

FOREWORD BY ROBERT SMITHER

McFarland & Company, Inc., Publishers
Jefferson, North Carolina, and London

Library of Congress Cataloguing-in-Publication Data

Halpern, Leslie, 1960–
    Dreams on film : the cinematic struggle between art and
science / by Leslie Halpern ; foreword by Robert Smither.
        p.   cm.
    Filmography: p.
    Includes bibliographical references and index.

    ISBN 0-7864-1596-7 (softcover : 50# alkaline paper)

    1. Dreams in motion pictures.   2. Dreams.   I. Title.
PN1995.9.D67H35   2003

                                                2002155759

British Library cataloguing data are available

On the cover: Scott Crowell in *Stranger* (Firebrand Films, 2000);
courtesy of Mr. Crowell.

Manufactured in the United States of America

McFarland & Company, Inc., Publishers
    Box 611, Jefferson, North Carolina 28640
        www.mcfarlandpub.com

Acknowledgments

My sincere appreciation extends to Gabriel Byrne, Henry Bromell, Ben Rock, Joel Hopkins, and Tunde Adebimpe, the filmmakers and actors who agreed to be interviewed for this book. A special thanks to filmmakers Alan Berliner, Scott Crowell, and Christian J. Otjen for also providing photographs of their work; Linda DiBattista, deputy arts & entertainment editor at *The Orlando Sentinel* for helping me locate photographs; and Sigrid and Philip Tiedtke and the rest of the gang at The Florida Film Festival for facilitating my research and bringing cutting-edge independent films (and filmmakers) to Central Florida.

Thanks also to reference librarian Bill Svitavsky at Rollins College's Olin Library and Professor Robert Smither, director of the Master of Liberal Studies Program at Rollins College for his readings, suggestions, and encouragement.

I also want to thank Steven Halpern for his technical and emotional support, and our son, Alexander, my ultimate wish fulfillment.

That's the thing about dreams. They're always right and always wrong.[1]

— Robert Downey, Jr., as serial killer and telepathic dream transmitter Vivian Thompson in *In Dreams* (1998)

Table of Contents

Foreword

I have spread my dreams under your feet;
Tread softly because you tread on my dreams.

— William Butler Yeats
He Wishes for the Cloths of Heaven (1899)

Down through the ages, people have turned to gypsies, prophets, poets, artists, psychologists, and others to help them make sense of their dreams. The most famous dream interpreter is, of course, Sigmund Freud. To the end of his life, Freud regarded his book *The Interpretation of Dreams* one of his greatest achievements. Even today, after traditional psychoanalysis has split into the schools of object relations, self psychology, interpersonal theory, ego psychology, and other variations, Freud's dream theory remains largely intact and still serves as the preferred framework for many dream interpreters.

Freud considered *The Interpretation of Dreams* significant because it was the first scientific effort to understand something that, so far as we know, all people experience. Today, however, Freudian theory is only one of several ways to interpret dreams, and those who wish to find the meaning of the images that come into consciousness during sleep can turn to Jungian theory, existential psychology, Gestalt therapy, or modern neurological theories of the dreaming process. Some neurological theories, in fact, can be used to argue that dreams have no meaning.

Although not everyone remembers dreams, all people have them, and certainly all people are familiar with dream sequences in movies. In filmic dreams, action moves into the consciousness of a sleeping character who sees a series of images that may or may not be comprehensible to the dreamer or the audience. These dream sequences serve many purposes. They can explain, confuse, scare, reassure, or give insights into someone's character. In many cases, in fact, dream sequences are the key to understanding the meaning of a film.

But as familiar as dream sequences may be to filmgoers, our knowledge of dreams on film remains sketchy. We know dreams often appear in films, but how frequently? Which of the dream theories most appeals to directors? Have movie dream sequences kept pace with modern dream research? Do the dreams we see on film accurately reflect our scientific knowledge of the dreaming process? And how do the dream sequences of classic films such as *Spellbound* compare with modern sequences in films such as *In Dreams* or even *Pee-wee's Big Adventure*?

In a creative approach to answering these questions, film expert Leslie Halpern has collected and analyzed more than one hundred examples of dreams on film. Her research suggests that as important as Hollywood regards the dream sequence, most directors do not "tread softly" on dreams as Yeats suggested. In fact, most directors don't seem to be bound by either dream theory or science. And in many cases, dream sequences are fashioned into a format that fits the director's purpose, irrespective of what science knows about dreams. Halpern asks the interesting question: Is this because directors and screenwriters don't understand dream theory or because filmmakers prefer artistic license to scientific reality?

Halpern has made an important contribution to our understanding of the linkage between dreams and film, showing us how directors use the universal experience of dreaming to further their own purposes in telling a specific story. Her work deepens our understanding of dreams on films and, at the same time, deepens our appreciation of both the movies we see on the screen and those private movies brought to us nightly by our unconscious.

Robert Smither
Professor of Psychology and Director,
Master of Liberal Studies Program,
Rollins College

Preface

Dream sequences leave me spellbound. In fact, the whole idea of the film as a public dream fascinates me. In terms of form, instead of a glass of warm milk, a darkened room, a cozy bed and closed eyes, the public dream usually begins with warm popcorn, a darkened room, plush stadium seating, and eyes wide open. In terms of content, films enable fleeting inner emotions with universal appeal to transcend time, place, and language through the permanent images of cinematic expression. Although a dream can only be remembered after the fact, a film can be watched over and over on videotape or DVD.

However, the most intriguing comparison between film and dream surrounds the "willing suspension of disbelief for the moment," a term coined by Romantic poet Samuel Taylor Coleridge in *Biographia Literaria* (1817) to describe the audience's faith in accepting the figurative truth in artistic imagination. Just as dreamers accept their own nightly visions as real *while they are asleep*, moviegoers accept the film's reality *while they are in the theater*. For the sake of art, we believe our filmic dream, temporarily forgetting the rumors of on-set romances and magazine articles alleging theft of intellectual property, and briefly overlooking predictable endings, continuity glitches, and embarrassing anachronisms.

When films include dream sequences, i.e., dreams within dreams, we must completely embrace the concept of suspending our disbelief. Films like *Total Recall* (1990), *Jacob's Ladder* (1990), and *Twelve Monkeys* (1995) take us into a character's dream while he or she is already in an altered state of consciousness, and we witness a dream within a dream within a dream, stretching the limits of Coleridge's theory.

Though not literally dreaming within a dream, Rob Reiner's *The Princess Bride* (1987) presents a similar situation. The overall framework of the film is a loving grandfather reading a fairy tale to his sick grandson. The fairy tale, which comprises the bulk of the film, surrounds a young

3

couple hopelessly in love and the vile prince who does everything he can to prevent their happiness. Within the fairy tale, Buttercup (Robin Wright), the lovely young woman sought by the hero and the villain, dreams that she marries the prince and faces the scorn of her subjects, thus creating a dream within a story within a dream.

Living in Oblivion (1994) is a low-budget independent film about the making of a low-budget independent film in which the director has great difficulty constructing a dream sequence, i.e., a dream within a dream within a dream with a twist.

In Cameron Crowe's *Vanilla Sky* (2001), a handsome publisher (Tom Cruise) awakens to find he is a disfigured prisoner who awakens to find he is a handsome publisher who awakens to find he is a disfigured prisoner who awakens to find.... This perplexing journey into the world of one man's nightmares is actually a dream within a dream within a dream within a dream.

So why all the subterfuge? Freud writes in *The Interpretation of Dreams* (1994), originally published in 1900, that the most abstracted level of a dream within a dream is the reality, while the continued dream (in this case, the film itself) is merely wish fulfillment. In other words, the deeper the dream is buried within layers of consciousness, the deeper its meaning to the dreamer. Films use dreams as a figurative means of revealing the literal truth hidden deep within the dreamer. With the exception of altered states of consciousness such as flashbacks, fantasies, and hallucinations, when film characters dream they also sleep. Our belief in the magic of motion pictures allows us to accept characters who fall asleep like they fall in love — easily, quickly, deeply, illogically, and in extremely uncomfortable positions.

Although sleep science, film technology, and audience sophistication have evolved tremendously during the past fifty or so years, the cinematic struggle between art and science in crafting the dream sequence remains virtually unchanged. So beginning with Alfred Hitchcock's 1945 psychological thriller *Spellbound*—filmed in the heyday of Freudian psychoanalytic dream theory just before the 1953 discovery of rapid eye movement (REM)—and continuing through the new breed of filmmakers cranking out features today, *Dreams On Film: The Cinematic Struggle Between Art and Science* examines this discrepancy.

I hate to ruin the ending for those who enjoy unexpected plot developments, but the secret to successful dream sequences — usually contained within equally successful films — relies on the audience's willing belief in the figurative truth of art overpowering the literal truth of science. Those of us who wholeheartedly believe in film as art would accept it no other way.

Introduction:
The Dream Sequence

I don't believe in dreams. That Freud stuff's a lot of hooey.

— Gregory Peck as amnesiac John Ballantine
in *Spellbound* (1945)

The unofficial filmmaker's formula for incorporating dreams into movies is quite simple: show ordinary people having extraordinary dreams. These dreams can use state-of-the-art technology to produce awe-inspiring visions that give insight into the character, promote the story, and provide emotional impact. However, when the smoke clears, the garbled sound returns to normal, the masks are removed, the makeup is washed off, and the lights come on, it becomes apparent that the reality of sleep science is sacrificed in order to save the illusion of the story.

In a dream sequence typical of most dreams on film, in the 1998 Neil Jordan thriller *In Dreams*, the camera comes in for a close-up of Claire Cooper (played by Annette Bening) as she drifts off to sleep under the influence of a heavy sedative prescribed by her psychiatrist. (She requires hospitalization and psychiatric care because of recurring nightmares). Her eyes, like her body, are perfectly still as she instantly transitions from a waking state to a dreaming state. A few seconds of total darkness precede a brief morphed image of Claire (as in clairvoyant) walking through her black and white dream in slow motion; all other colors are muted with low key lighting except for the bright red drape and lipstick that she wears.

Each scene fades into another as Claire wanders down lonely streets through a nearly deserted town. A dog howls in the distant background, soft music underscores the scene, and children play alongside the road. Claire follows an unknown path, guided by an unseen force. She enters the abandoned Carlton Hotel where hallways are filled with mysterious fog which has no apparent purpose or source of origin. Suddenly the earlier sound of a barking dog transforms into fierce snarling that grows louder as she follows her predetermined path. As she approaches room 401 the growling becomes more threatening. She enters the unlocked room and discovers her dead husband (Aidan Quinn) lying on the floor, his face crushed and covered with bright red blood as a rabid dog looms over him. The music, howling, and wailing increase in volume and intensity until the dream abruptly ends.

Claire awakens in a crazed terror; she remembers every detail of the dream — including the exact hotel and room number — and is fully cognizant of its underlying meaning: her husband's life is in danger from a psychopath who lives in an orchard full of red apples. Later, however, serial killer Vivian Thompson (Robert Downey, Jr.) takes great delight in correcting Claire's misinterpretation of her dreams when he finally meets her in person, after killing her daughter and husband, kidnapping a girl named "Ruby" and invading Claire's dreams telepathically. He lives in an apple cider factory, not an apple orchard.

Filled with rich sensory stimulation including a soft focus, special lighting effects, disturbing sound effects, and eerie musical distortion,

Claire Cooper (Annette Bening) roams through the hallways of the abandoned Carlton Hotel in a telepathic nightmare from the horror film *In Dreams* (Dream-Works Pictures, 1998). Photograph by Francois Duhamel.

Claire's dream is packed with meaning integral to the film's plot. Her dream also is packed with technical inaccuracies and physical impossibilities contrary to recent findings of neuroscience. Instead, the dream remains faithful to early twentieth century dream theories such as Freud's five dreamwork processes of displacement (redirecting thoughts, emotions, or urges from one person/object to another), condensation (merging people or places), symbolization (representing a repressed urge with a symbol), projection (moving our repressed desires onto other people), and secondary revision (constructing a story that connects the various elements during the final stage of the dream process), and Carl Gustav Jung's idea of a collective unconscious with a pool of shared images. This particular dream sequence reveals the deepest fears of the dreamer, the inner workings of the psychotic character's unconscious mind, and an unavoidable prophesy. In short, it reveals the art, rather than the science, of dreaming.

This cinematic struggle between art and science is not limited to psychological thrillers such as *In Dreams,* which relies on dreams to explore characters' emotional problems. Films about dreams and films using dreams cut across the boundaries of time, genre, and budget. Characters have dreams, talk about dreams, remember dreams, simulate dreams, lie about dreams, and transmit dreams with amazing frequency and even more amazing inaccuracy in terms of scientific form and content. Often disguised through not-so-subtle poetic imagery, dream sequences—and the sleep cycles that precede and follow them —count on our willingness to forget about the scientific knowledge in our heads and rely on the emotions in our hearts.

Actor-producer Gabriel Byrne, whose career spans three decades and includes more than forty films and several dream and dreamlike sequences, says the emotional aspect of dreams on film emanates from their ability to reflect the world around us.

> Films and dreams mirror our reality, especially the deeply felt areas of our lives which give us fear, joy, anticipation, or puzzlement. Dreams are like movies played out in our sleep and movies are like dreams played out on a blank wall in a dark room for a mass audience.... The whole process of film is hallucination and dreams. Just like dreams, films reflect back our own subconscious reality and thereby teach us about who we are and what kind of lives we live.[2]

It may be hard to imagine the Dublin-born actor having much in common with the characters he has portrayed, including lawyers, priests, gangsters, cowboys, gypsies, and the devil. Yet Byrne, whose credits include *The Usual Suspects (1995), Miller's Crossing (1990),* and his 1981 debut in

Excalibur, says each character reflects part of himself, in addition to mirroring society at large. The personal quality of this mass medium makes films the perfect setting for entering a dreamlike state of consciousness.

Characters including lawyers, priests, gangsters, cowboys, gypsies, and even the devil become more understandable, more accessible, and more real to us by sneaking a peek into their subconscious. Dream sequences intensify our relationships with film characters. "In dreams for which narrative cues and preparation are provided, our cinematic dream screens become doubly charged sites of that part of the oneiric [dream interpretation] narrative. Many techniques used by filmmakers to convey certain sensations in dreams can appeal with special force to us as viewers" because we know how it feels to fall, fly, fear, love, and desire in our dreams (Eberwein, 1984, 192).

These feelings revealed in cinematic dreams may not always be understandable to the audience on a conscious level. In filmed images of any kind, "a conscious standpoint is directly juxtaposed with visualizations of the realities and potentialities of the unconscious itself. Rarely in other art forms are conscious and unconscious elements given such equal emotional weight by being viewed as parts of a common frame" (Beebe, 1996, 580). Repeated viewings of Alfred Hitchcock or Ingmar Bergman films, for example, may bring new conscious insights each time, but the unconscious emotions associated with the films and their dream sequences likely remain the same.

Some films go beyond brief dream sequences into another realm: the dream film, in which the visual aspect of cinema conveys a subliminal story through unique logic and seemingly irrational images that cannot be entirely verbalized. "Because you give as much as you take, you somehow meet dream films on a common ground somewhere in your subconscious" (Thompson, 1990, 68). Directors such as Tim Burton, Ken Russell, and Terry Gilliam routinely direct dark, dreamlike films that create their own rules of logic and laws of nature, and often include dream sequences within the dreamlike structure of the story.

Although modern sleep scientists understand how we dream, they still know little about why. This lack of knowledge about the function of the dreaming mind does not stand in the way of good filmmaking, however. Unabashedly emphasizing the unknown psychological elements over the known physiological ones, filmed dream sequences manipulate or sacrifice scientific form and content in order to express the director's creative vision and keep the audiences coming back for more.

The independent feature film *Stranger* (2000) includes a nonlinear blend of hallucinatory, flashback, and dream sequences to convey the disturbed mind of the central character, an unnamed drifter who is a self-described "giver of life and a taker." Scott Crowell, who directed, wrote, produced, edited, and starred in the film, echoes the words of other directors who say they have never studied, read, or heard anything at film school about how to create a dream sequence. "It's just burned into our psyches how to make a dream sequence by watching so many films that have them," he says. "Although most filmmakers try to do something different each time, they are always copying off other people and developing those ideas. The same is true with dream sequences."[3]

Nor is the struggle between the art and science of dreams on film anything new. Since George Eastman produced the first celluloid roll film in America in 1884 and the Lumière brothers opened the first movie theater in France in 1895, filmmakers have experimented with the depiction of dreams on film, with more than two hundred pre–World War I French and American short silent films involving dreams (Gamwell, 2000). The earliest documented dream sequence — a prophetic dream appearing in a circular inset called a dream balloon — was used in Edwin Porter's 1903 film *The Life of an American Fireman* (Robards, 1991). The mid-twentieth century continued the exploration of film and dream with psychological thrillers such as *Spellbound* (1945), which begins with the words:

> Our story deals with psychoanalysis, the method by which modern science treats the emotional problems of the sane. The analyst seeks only to induce the patient to talk about his hidden problems, to open the locked doors of his mind. Once the complexes that have been disturbing the patient are uncovered and interpreted, the illness and confusion disappear ... and the devils of unreason are driven from the human soul.

The key to opening the locked doors of the mind and driving out those unreasonable devils is, of course, a dream, which comes near the end of the film.

Even today, despite other creative tools and technological capabilities available to filmmakers, the dream sequence remains a popular device for meeting a variety of artistic needs: an opening dream immediately establishes what the character is feeling; a later dream or series of dreams warns us of the impending climax; and a concluding dream ties the loose ends. This lasting preoccupation with dreams on film likely reflects peoples' inherent interest in escaping from their own problems and peeking into someone else's mind.

Ben Rock, production designer for *The Blair Witch Project* (1999) and director of the telefilm *The Burkittsville 7* (2000), supports Crowell's claim that dream sequences never made the syllabus on any of his courses in college. "We never studied dream sequences in film school, and no one ever taught me how to do a dream sequence. I don't ever remember talking about dream sequences," Rock says. "You couldn't write a book on how to make a dream sequence because it's a very personal bias."[4] Luckily, the focus here is on *why*, rather than *how*. Why is science lost or distorted in the process of representing dreams on film, and why do we prefer this figurative truth of art over the literal truth of science in this representation?

PART I

Technical Difficulties: Changes in Form

JAY: Hey Zed, doesn't anybody ever get any sleep around here?

ZED: The twins keep us on Centurian time. It's a thirty-seven-hour day. Give it a few months, you'll get used to it — or you'll have a psychotic episode.

> — Jay (Will Smith) to Zed (Rip Torn)
> as a top-secret government operative investigating
> alien visitations on earth in *Men in Black* (1997)

Chapter 1

History of Dream Theory

In *Marnie* (1964), Tippi Hedren plays Margaret Edgar, a pathological liar who also suffers from kleptomania, frigidity, and recurring nightmares. When millionaire businessman and amateur zoologist Mark Rutland (Sean Connery) tries to help her, one of the first things he does is interpret her dreams. Mistakenly convinced that her dreams mean nothing, Margaret says sarcastically, "You Freud, me Jane." In films, non-credentialed armchair Freudians like Rutland frequently interpret dreams with amazing accuracy.

However, accurate dream interpretation is not quite so easy and it did not begin with Sigmund Freud. Tracing the roots of dream interpretation, however, allows us to see how Freud and Carl Gustav Jung, two of the most respected and published psychiatrists devoted to dreamwork, based their new ideas on old traditions. Since ancient times, people have wondered about the source and content of their dreams because determining where dreams come from is crucial to interpreting their meaning. From the great thinkers in ancient Greece through the early church fathers of the Middle Ages, dreams were viewed as divine gifts or messages from demons and devils. Five thousand years ago, the ancients practiced dream incubation, in which a request for a dream explanation is made to ourselves, to God, to the dead or to the universal forces once known as gods and goddesses. "Dream incubation encompasses life in every respect so by having the right dream at the right time it can help with practical, down-to earth problems just as easily as it can bring flashes of enlightenment and inspiration from heavenly heights" (Dee, 1984, 10). The ancients also believed that Sleep and his brother, Death, dwelt in the lower world from which dreams ascended to man. "[Dreams] passed through two gates, one of horn through which true dreams went, one of ivory for false dreams" (Hamilton, 1969, 40).

Dreams as Religious Expressions

Hippocrates, the early Greek father of medicine, suggested that "Some dreams are divinely inspired, but others are the result of the physical body" (Dee, 1984, 16). Even so, the majority of ancient Greeks and Romans believed dreams originate from various gods and goddesses, and were therefore far more concerned with interpretation of their nightly visions than in tracking down their source. "In ancient Greece and Rome, for example, dream interpreters actually accompanied military leaders into battle, so essential was the understanding of dream content" (Koch-Sheras and Lemley, 1995, 24). Dreams have always influenced religious belief and conduct, politics and battle decisions, medical treatment, and personal decisions in time of crisis. "At least from the dawn of recorded history, people were compelled to interpret the meaning of the stories and images in their dreams. In fact, in centuries past, societies invested dreams with even more power and importance than the experiences of their waking lives" (Koch-Sheras and Lemley, 1995, 24). Dreams are powerful, important and accessible, offering a free potential source of wisdom and guidance to every person regardless of age, race, sex, education, socioeconomic bracket, or level of spiritual development. Dreams and their interpretation also abound throughout the Old and New Testaments, with prophetic dreams guiding the most powerful kings to the lowest of slaves (see Chapter 10).

The practice of dream interpretation came under disfavor by early church fathers, however. "Whereas some cultures embraced dream life as an important dimension, worthy of interpretation and exploration, Western Christian culture emphasized only the most literal or transparently symbolic interpretations, so threatened was that culture by the possibility that dream content might undermine the morality being handed down by the Church. Despite numerous biblical references to dream interpretation, the practice was discouraged as frivolous, if not dangerous, perhaps influenced by the early Christian belief that dreams were sent by the devil" (Koch-Sheras and Lemley, 1995, 41). With church fathers denouncing all dreams not deemed as divine revelations experienced by a man of God, "It is clear to see how this ignorant indoctrination made its mark on society generally, with the very word 'dream' being changed to mean not a vision in the night but a forlorn hope" (Dee, 1984, 25).

In the Middle Ages, the influential thirteenth century priest St. Thomas Aquinas also had opinions about dreams and their relationship to the Catholic Church. St. Thomas tried to discount the possibility that dreams have special meaning, attributing them to three different causes: waking experiences, physical sensations, and the work of God or demons.

"While he did not believe it was sinful to interpret the first two types of dreams, as earlier Christians had held, he did consider it 'unlawful and superstitious' to derive meaning from dreams sent by demons" (Koch-Sheras and Lemley, 1995, 30).

St. Thomas wrote extensively about the prophetic nature of dreams, suggesting a "'single cause of both the dream and the event,' a concept reminiscent of Jung's synchronicity" (Dee, 1984, 25). "In considering the question of divination in dreams, Aquinas refers to the passage in Deuteronomy 18:10, 'Let there not be found among you him who observes dreams,' which had been mistranslated by Jerome. Aquinas concluded that divination would not be unlawful if dreams proceeded from divine revelation or natural causes" (Van De Castle, 1994, 80).

Dreams came under increasing review by sixteenth century philosophers and scientists who created new theories of dream analysis based on purely physical functioning. Years later, the scientific revolution inspired more theories about the functionality of dreaming until Freud's *The Interpretation of Dreams* (1900) increased interest in the study of repressed desires of the unconscious mind revealed through dreams. In his groundbreaking book, Freud popularizes the idea of a manifest (literal) and latent (symbolic) content of dreams that appear to the unconscious self during sleep, thus freeing the dreamer from neuroses caused by repressed fears or desires, often originating in childhood.

The purpose of dreams, he proposes, is to satisfy through fantasy our socially unacceptable instinctual urges. He believes that strictly internal sources create dreams messages from the unconscious that express "day residues" or rehashes of events in waking life, as well as repressions and unfulfilled wishes often of a sexual nature. Dreams are coded messages—highly condensed, richly symbolic expressions of unconscious wish fulfillment — that function as tools for the psychoanalyst in building better mental health for the patient, according to Freud.

Dreams as Psychological Expressions

Under his tutelage, doctors and patients began viewing dreams as psychological expressions, rather than religious or prophetic ones. God, the devil and other external sources of origin were de-emphasized while new emphasis was placed on Freud's concept of a personal trinity, the id, ego and super-ego (Dee, 1984). In 1900, *The Interpretation of Dreams* also foreshadowed the discovery of REM (rapid eye movement) sleep with Freud's observation that "motor paralysis during sleep is one of the fundamental conditions of the psychic process which functions during dreaming" (Freud, 1994, 227). In an effort to understand the function of dreams, he studied, observed, and theorized about dream formation and their application in treating mental illness, thus for the first time promoting clinical respectability toward the study of dreams. Freud's empirical findings are the foundation for countless physiological studies, inspired by the desire to prove — or more often disprove — his two fundamental theories that dreaming preserves sleep and discharges instinctual drives or basic wishes, usually of a sexual or aggressive nature, that are disturbing to the individual when awake.

Among Freud's most famous concepts outlined in the book — and certainly his most popular among filmmakers — is his sexual symbolization in dreams. "It is quite true that symbolizations of the bodily organs and functions do occur in dreams: for example, that water in a dream often signifies a desire to urinate, that the male genital organ may be represented by an upright staff, or pillar, etc." (Freud, 1994, 127). The huge rock formation in *Picnic at Hanging Rock* (1975), Freddy Krueger's knives in *A Nightmare on Elm Street* (1984), and the speeding train in one of the *Dreamscape* (1984) dreams serve as just a few of many possible examples of sexual symbols thrust upon us by filmmakers. Freud also opened the floodgates for a vast amount of watery dream sequences when he noted that "a large number of dreams, which are frequently full of anxiety, and often have for content the traversing of narrow spaces, or staying long in the water, are based upon phantasies concerning the intra-uterine life, the sojourn in the mother's womb, and the act of birth" (271). *Rosemary's Baby* (1968) and *In Dreams* (1998) combine dreamy images of water with scenes of death, motherhood, and violence. *The Story of Adele H.* (1975) and *Ordinary People* (1980) feature recurrent dreams about drowned siblings.

Slightly less popular are Freud's theories of locations as symbols. "There are dreams of landscapes and localities in which emphasis is always laid upon the assurance: 'I have been here before.' But this 'Déjà vu' has a special significance in dreams. In this case the locality is always the genitals of the mother; of no other place can it be asserted with such certainty that one 'has been there before'" (Freud, 1994, 271). In *The Mummy Returns* (2001), librarian Evelyn (Rachel Weisz) visits an ancient archeological site with her explorer husband, Rick O'Connell (Brendan Fraser). She experiences visions inside the temple that give her a feeling of déjà vu. Certain she has been there before, but unable to explain it, Evelyn finds her answer at the end of the film. Though her revelation does deal with her youth and ancestry, it has little (if any) direct connection to her mother's genitals.

Jung, a former Freudian disciple, later developed his own ideas about

Evelyn O'Connell (Rachel Weisz, right) experiences déjà vu when she has visions of herself in an ancient cat fight while visiting a temple with her husband, Ric (Brendan Fraser), in *The Mummy Returns* (Universal Pictures, 2001). Photograph by Keith Hamshere.

dreams, promoting archetypes—universal images with mythological significance — that devote far less attention to what he considered unhealthy sexual repression. Instead of wish fulfillment, Jung says dreams serve as a balance, compensating for under-represented parts of the personality in waking life. Jung favors a spiritual message from the collective unconscious, yet agrees with Freud's belief that dreams serve the function of revealing inner turmoil. "Dreams give information about the secrets of the inner life and reveal to the dreamer hidden factors of his personality. As long as these are undiscovered, they disturb his waking life and betray themselves only in the form of symptoms" (Jung, 1933, 16).

Like Freud, Jung also strives to bring dream theory out of the Dark Ages when dreams supposedly originated from devils and demons. "The dream is a natural event and there is no reason under the sun why we should assume that it is a crafty device to lead us astray," he writes in *Psychology and Religion* (1938, 31). Even so, dreams—with their dubious origins and shaded meanings—continue to arouse suspicion even today because of their symbolic expression and occasional precognitive glimpses of the future.

According to Jung, dreams go beyond expressing fears and desires, tapping into all kinds of spiritual, emotional and mental potential, revealing the collective unconscious, mankind's pool of shared dream images. "Even dreams are made of collective material to a very high degree, just as, in the mythology and folklore of different peoples, certain motives repeat themselves in almost identical form" (Jung, 1938, 63). His archetypes are based on the idea that common dream symbols transcend time.

Dreams as Filmic Expressions

Independent filmmaker Alan Berliner taps into this collective unconscious through his experimental, documentary, and essay films that combine found footage with his enormous archives of sounds and photos. "Those images, sounds, and memories have a collective power over all of us ... as civilization evolves moment by moment, through the drama of human discourse that we all share. It's a question of linking the big universe of information ('the world') with the small universe of information ('the mind'). One feeds the other in a kind of endless loop."[5] His films, including *The Sweetest Sound* (2001), rely on a tacit universal understanding of these archetypes in order to evoke personal responses in the viewer.

This endless loop also applies to television movies and series. Martin Esslin writes in *The Age of Television*:

> The pantheon of archetypal characters in ever-recurring situations on present day American television does ... reflect the collective psyche, the collective fears and aspirations, neuroses and nightmares of the average American, as distinct from the factual reality of the state of the nation ... These programs may present caricatures of real situations, but, like all good caricature and all myth, they merely intensify and enlarge the true features of the daydreams from which they spring. These then are the collective daydreams of this culture [1982, 44].

Man's fear of growing older and facing death, for example, is characterized on television and in the movies by Pee-wee Herman (Paul Reubens), a skinny man-child with a bad haircut, red bow tie, shiny white shoes, and ill-fitting suit. He lives alone, yet does not work; he is surrounded by friends, but does nothing to earn their friendship. Riding around town on his prized vintage bicycle, Pee-wee shows off for children in the neighborhood and honks the horn as he competes in imaginary races. Essentially, he is a grownup who refuses to grow up. From *Pee-wee's*

Playhouse on television to *Pee-wee's Big Adventure* at the movie theater, the character symbolizes our collective need to hope, play, pretend, and dream at any age.

Freud's concept of repressions and wishes in dreams and Jung's common dream symbols have transcended time — at least on film.

The conceptual schemata originated by Freud in *The Interpretation of Dreams* seems particularly apt for application to the art of film.... Freudian theory can illuminate the transformation from printed page to screened imagery and, by revealing certain

More than just a man-child and his machine, Pee-wee Herman (Paul Reubens) represents our collective need to hope, play, pretend, and dream in *Pee-wee's Big Adventure* (Warner Bros., 1985).

characteristic types of ambiguity, help to explain the power of that imagery, particularly, its ability to convey economically a vast range of meaning [Spitz, 1991, 205].

Within the scientific community, in the mid-twentieth century the theoretical concepts of Freud, Jung, and other early dream pioneers suddenly became secondary to empirical case studies of the sleep scientists. This revolution in science, however, had (and continues to have) little impact on the depiction of dreams on film which hold tight to the intriguing sexual and violent content of Freudian theory and the universality of Jungian ideas.

The lack of literal truth in dreams on film reflects an overall lack of literal truth in film. Other than documentaries, which strive for accuracy despite an inevitable filmmaker agenda, narrative films combine the known and unknown, real and imagined, and ordinary and extraordinary to appeal to various audiences at various levels of interpretation. "In the psychological analysis of a film, its documentary aspect may be usefully taken as a gloss for what Jung spoke of as the conscious or ego 'standpoint' toward a situation; the dream aspect would then correspond to the attitude of the unconscious. I believe that the most interesting films deal with the interaction of the documentary with the dream level" (Beebe, 1996, 581). Because this unconscious dream level relies on figurative truth to make its point, audiences will forgive a few technical inaccuracies if the film's message conveys emotional integrity.

In fact, the revolution in technology is of far more interest to filmmakers than the revolution in science. High-tech cameras, digital technology, and computer-generated images make it easier and more interesting to produce dreamlike effects. Dreams can be introduced by shots of the sleeper followed by the dream, distortions in sound, fades, dissolves, superimpositions, or dozens of other filmmaker tricks to establish an altered state of consciousness. Throughout the dream sequence, intercuts of the sleeper remind us that it's only a dream. "In whatever form the filmmaker chooses to present the dream, we understand it as a psychic projection of a mind made visible on the screen. At the moment that the dream appears, we enter into a new phenomenological relationship with the cinematic screen and with the dreaming mind represented there" (Eberwein, 1984, 53). Films that lack these cues, *Persona* (1966), *Belle de Jour* (1967), *Picnic at Hanging Rock* (1975), *Shattered Image* (1998), and *Vanilla Sky* (2001) for example, intentionally challenge viewers to make their own determinations about what is dream and what is reality. Whether or not they manifestly present dream sequences or cleverly blur the lines of dream and reality, filmmakers care little about new scientific information on dream physiology, instead focusing their attention (and cameras) on older, more artistic concepts of dream psychology that address a figurative kind of truth.

Chapter 2

Physiology of Sleeping and Dreaming

In the horror film, *A Nightmare on Elm Street* (1984), teenaged Nancy Thompson (Heather Langenkamp) is taken to a sleep laboratory so doctors can study her recurring nightmares about a razor-clawed killer who stalks her in dreams. "I don't see why you couldn't just give me a pill to keep me from dreaming," she tells the doctor. He looks at her sympathetically. "Everyone's got to dream, young lady. If you don't dream you go..." he says, while encircling his head with a pen to represent "crazy." Although modern science has not invented a pill specifically designed to stop dreams, nor have any cases of insanity been attributed solely to lack of dreaming, the scene accurately taps into universal concerns about sleep that have been with us since antiquity.

Born around 540 B.C., the ancient Greek philosopher Heraclitus of Ephesus claimed that despite an independent, objective truth available to everyone (Logos), the majority of people live in their own private dream world in which they sleepwalk through life. Of the few dozen remaining fragments of his philosophies, many examine altered states of consciousness. Heraclitus writes, "For the waking there is one common world, but when asleep each person turns away to a private one," acknowledging a clear distinction between the mind's accessibility when waking and sleeping (Cohen, Curd, Reeve, 1995, 27, frag.22).

Heraclitus also explored how an inactive body works in conjunction with an active mind at rest, believing that the sleeping mind represents motion, rather than a lifeless depository for messages from the gods or a deathlike state until the body awakens. Though motionless, physical and mental processes continue: The body grows and ages; the mind shifts and sorts ideas. Heraclitus answers the age-old question of how we can wake up in the morning after a full night's sleep and still be tired: "Changing, it rests," he writes (Cohen, Curd, Reeve, 1995, 31, frag.75). This paradox is actually a valid explanation for the constant motion of life, even during the sleep from which we can be awakened.

Amazingly, these ancient ideas are echoed in the science of today. Sleep expert William C. Dement, who founded the world's first sleep disorders center in 1970 at Stanford University, says the two defining traits of sleep are (1) the erection of a perceptual wall between the conscious mind and stimuli from the outside world, and (2) the immediate reversibility of sleep when the sleeper is awakened (Dement and Vaughan, 1999).

The Discovery of REM

Today's understanding of sleep and dreams, however, was preceded by revelations in the not-too-distant past. What Freud did for understanding the psychology of dreaming with the publication of *The Interpretation of Dreams* in 1900, Eugene Aserinsky and Nathaniel Kleitman did for understanding the physiological aspects of dreaming with the discovery of REM in 1953. Aserinsky, a graduate student of physiology working with Kleitman at the University of Chicago, noticed that during the night, the eyes of sleeping subjects moved rapidly beneath closed lids, and when awakened during these rapid eye movements, twenty out of twenty-seven test subjects recalled vivid dreams. Aserinky's interviews with people awakened during ocular inactivity resulted in nineteen out of twenty-three people with no dream recall whatsoever (Madow and Snow, 1970). This discovery prompted the establishment of sleep laboratories around the world to study this phenomenon.

In the sci-fi thriller *Dreamscape* (1984), the fictional government-funded sleep laboratory at Thornhill College that researches sleep disorders, sexual dysfunction, and dream-linking in its sleep-monitoring stations is based on actual laboratories. The film's credits include a medical advisor whose assistance helps maintain the scientific integrity of scenes depicting initiation of REM, brain wave patterns, and heart-monitoring systems, making *Dreamscape*— despite its frequent leaps of artistic faith — one of the most scientifically accurate dream movies. Real sleep laboratories may indeed have technicians monitoring the patient's breathing, heart rate, oxygen saturation, eye movements, and genital response.

The outcome of numerous sleep studies in the mid and late 1900s produced a wealth of empirical data about sleep and the approximately two hours we spend dreaming each night. Four identifiable stages of sleep occur during ninety-minute sleep cycles, which repeat throughout the night. The transitional stage of passing into sleep is Stage 1, which lasts up to ten minutes and is not repeated. Transient sleep experienced in Stage 2 for twenty minutes up to forty-five minutes is followed by Stages 3 and 4 where the deepest sleep occurs for a few minutes or up to an hour.

> The sleeper eventually returns to Stage 2 sleep, and then enters a REM state, typically for a few minutes. At this point, the sleeper has completed the first sleep cycle. After the initial REM state, the sleeper goes back to Stage 2 sleep, repeating the entire sequence all over again (with the absence of Stage 1 sleep, which is more of a transitional state that an actual sleep stage). In each succeeding cycle, the duration of REM sleep (in which most dreaming occurs) becomes longer and longer, until by morning REM periods can last as long as an hour [Lewis, 1995, 226].

Dreaming occurs during NREM (non–REM, synchronized, or orthodox) sleep which produces dream images resembling neurotic thought loops (Did I lock the door? I know I locked the door. Did I lock the door?) and REM (desynchronized or paradoxical) sleep which produces dreams with psychotic scenes that defy logic, reason, and laws of nature (a snake-man monster enters through the unlocked door and flies around the house).

The stages of sleep are necessary biological adaptations for restorative and conservatory processes, such as pituitary growth hormone levels, which peak during NREM sleep, promoting protein synthesis in the cerebral cortex, the retina, and throughout the body that aid in cell growth and tissue repair. During NREM sleep when eyes are still, the body is relaxed, brain waves are slowed, and dreams are bland, the dreamer may experience tossing and turning, sleepwalking (somnambulism), night terrors, moaning, and sleeptalking (somniloquy).

After about an hour of NREM sleep, the brain stem is activated by neurochemical changes that start sending impulses to higher brain regions, thus activating REM. "During REM sleep, the area in the brain stem containing the bulbar reticular formation neurons sends hyperpolarizing signals to the spinal cord, blocking external sensory input and motor output" (Flanagan, 2000, 16). In reaction, the heart rate increases, breathing becomes shallow, and twitching may be present in the face, fingers, and toes. Movement in NREM sleep is episodic and involuntary, while REM movement is voluntary but inhibited. Despite similar brain waves during waking and REM, the body experiences external paralysis in REM sleep with only the eyes and respiratory system remaining fully functional.

Dream Paralysis

Most people have experienced paralysis in a dream. Being unable to scream, run away, or fight back against an attacker are common occurrences in REM sleep because at some level we know that we are paralyzed when we dream (Lewis, 1995). Because of this disconnection of the motor impulses, sleepwalking only occurs during non–REM sleep. Although a frustrating condition while we dream, REM paralysis is commonly believed to be an inherited safety mechanism passed from one generation to the next in order to prevent us from endangering ourselves by physically acting out the dramas of our dreams.

Subtle physiological changes during REM sleep are accompanied by more obvious signs. Genital arousal in healthy men and women is evident during REM sleep, which may have led Freud to incorrectly connect deep sleep with sexual dreams. "Experiments have shown that if subjects are woken repeatedly from REM sleep, the erection cycle will get out of phase with the REM cycle, so there is not necessarily a cause-and-effect relationship between the two phenomena" (Melbourne and Hearne, 1997, 18). Penile erections (also called nocturnal penile tumescence or NPT) during REM do not violate the rule about paralysis because the sexual excitation relates to blood engorgement rather than muscle action. Sleep laboratory studies have shown that the "increase in blood flow in both men and women during REM sleep is probably an incidental effect of the activation of the part of the autonomic nervous system that controls heart rate and other involuntary body functions" (Dement and Vaughan, 1999, 295). Similarly, orgasm during REM sleep is possible because the action is a reflex independent of the skeletal muscles.

The fictional sleep laboratory in *Dreamscape* also studies incidences of nocturnal penile tumescence in order to determine whether impotency has physical or psychological causes. Not surprisingly, the serious subject is treated lightly on film, as evidenced by a scene from *Dreamscape*.

"So what goes on in this section?" asks psychic dream-linker Alex Gardner (Dennis Quaid), who can predict the outcome of horse races, enter people's dreams, and read minds.

"Well, one of our areas of research is sexual dysfunction. If a man is experiencing impotency, we can determine whether the cause is physiological or psychological by monitoring his sleep," explains Dr. Jane DeVries (Kate Capshaw).

"How's that?" asks Alex.

"Well, if it isn't physical, he'll experience three or four erections during the course of the night."

Alex Gardner (Dennis Quaid) learns that the dream lab at Thornhill College studies more than nocturnal penile tumescence when he dream-links with a construction worker having a nightmare about a skyscraper in *Dreamscape* (20th Century–Fox, 1983).

"I see. So Jane, what you do here in effect is count boners."

She replies, "I can see you're going to be a real challenge to work with."

REM sleep, including temporary paralysis of everything except the heart, lungs, eyes, and genitals, is nearly universal among mammals, but adapts itself to their particular lives. "Evolution has made an incredible effort to restructure the brain many times to keep REM and non–REM sleep, and to shape it in different modes. Walking, standing up, changes in posture: the pattern varies, but still we find REM and non–REM sleep. The appearance of the same basic state in many multiple forms indicates that there is something very important here, because evolution did not let any mammal except for the anteater, lose it" (The Dalai Lama, 1997, 34).

The question still rages on whether or not dreaming is an evolutionary adaptation that increases biological fitness. In 1859, Charles Darwin wrote in *The Origin of Species*: "This preservation of favorable individual differences and variations, and the destruction of those which are injurious, I have called Natural Selection, or the Survival of the Fittest. Variations neither useful nor injurious would not be affected by natural selection, and would be left either a fluctuating element, as perhaps we see in certain polymorphic species, or would ultimately become fixed, owing to the nature of the organism and the nature of the conditions" (Darwin, 51). The question is, Do dreams promote biological fitness?

The answer is, probably not. Modern science usually views dreams as the "fluctuating elements" unaffected by natural selection. As defined in *The Quark and the Jaguar* (1994), the concept of biological fitness is "that propagation of genes from one generation to the next depends on survival of the organism until it reaches the stage of reproduction, followed by the generation of a reasonable number of offspring that in turn survive to produce" (Gell-Mann, 249). Therefore, adaptation requires that traits arise due to selection pressures—heritable traits will be modified over generations due to differential reproductive success of the organisms that possess the traits. Films such as *Altered States* (1980) explore the relationship of dreams to biological fitness through a man's mental (and eventually physical) journey back to primordial man during a series of dreams and visions experienced in an isolation tank.

Dreams and Biological Fitness

If related to adaptation, dreams would be functionally relevant to man's three distinguishing adaptive achievements—technology, social organization, and language—but no relevance is apparent (Jones, 1970). "No evidence has yet been found to support that human or animal paralysis during REM sleep occurs as a result of evolution and it seems unreasonable to assume that, by a quirky accident of nature, a few of our ancestors developed this ability and were the only ones who survived, their genes eventually being passed on to the rest of humanity" (Melbourne and Hearne, 1997, 19).

Still, as Dement, notes in his essay "A Sleep Researcher's Odyssey: The Function and Clinical Significance of REM Sleep," such an important issue is not dismissed easily.

> It is often possible to deduce the functional role or purpose of a biological phenomenon from a description of its properties... If this is a rule, REM sleep is the exception. Complete bafflement has been the usual result of a prolonged encounter with the problem of its existence and unique attributes. Nonetheless, a phenomenon that is so ubiquitous, so complex, and so well represented in terms of brain areas allocated to its mechanisms, is not likely to have evolved only as a capricious whim of Mother Nature. Although we are appealing to teleology, the pre-emptiveness of REM sleep under certain conditions, plus its anatomical, biochemical, and physiological complexity,

inspires an unshakable faith that REM sleep does have a vital biological role to play, and that we will eventually be able to describe this role with precision and profit [Dement, 1970, 81].

Similarly, Edward O. Wilson writes in *Consilience* (1998), "Biological capacity evolves until it maximizes the fitness of organisms for the niches they fill, and not a squiggle more" (48). Not falling within the realm of fitness maximization, perhaps dreams fill a different niche: The dreaming mind may have an emotionally adaptive function, yet not be a biological adaptation. "The distinction between intellectual and emotional insight is familiar to all psychotherapists. It refers to the difference between knowing the solution to a problem and making it a part of oneself, i.e., adaptation. It may be the latter process which occurs during REM sleep" (Pearlman, 1970, 330).

Emotionally adaptive traits are transmitted through a "process whereby the ego creates new organizations of the ideal state of the self to preserve the feeling of safety and to avoid the experience of being traumatically overwhelmed" (Pearlman, 1970, 332). In this case, successful adaptation involves the "continual relinquishing of ideals (wishes) which are no longer appropriate to present reality" (332). The post-traumatic nightmare, such as many Americans experienced after the September 11, 2001, terrorist attacks, is an example of unsuccessful functioning of the adaptive mechanism. In *Dreaming Souls*, Owen Flanagan writes that dream function can be seen as a nonadaptive side effect of sleep with indeterminate psychological benefits "constructed via mechanisms of individual and cultural imagination" (2000, 140). This function is based on the self-expressiveness of dreams, which may help constitute self-identity, self-knowledge, and personal growth.

The emotional component of sleep is described in *The Promise of Sleep:* "The logical part of the awake brain knows that the dream was not real, but the emotional part of the brain cannot set it aside. As far as our brains are concerned, what we dream really happens to us" (Dement and Vaughan, 1999, 292). Our dreams seem real, not because they make sense or relate to some external reality, but because they feel real while occurring and sometimes even afterwards. While awake, our stimulation comes from mostly external stimuli; while asleep, our stimulation comes almost exclusively from internal stimuli.

Even with this emotional aspect of dreaming, upon awakening, most of us have little trouble determining whether our experiences are real or dreamed. "The reason we commonly mistake our dreams for reality, but rarely mistake reality for a dream, is that it is easier to imagine one's embodiment in a world one dreams than to doubt one's embodiment in a world one shares with others. And yet, such doubts were voiced repeatedly in the philosophy and poetry of the seventeenth and eighteenth centuries, and well into the next, with both exhilarating and disturbing effects on the poet's perception of the world, self, and others" (Rzepka, 1986, 2). If we are lucky enough to remember our dreams, we can incorporate their self-expressive function for personal development or merely laugh about our strange dream when we retell it to our friends.

REM sleep and dreaming may not play a large role in human biological adaptation, but dreams often play a significant role in the movies, and undergo their own adaptations by filmmakers who alter sleep science for the sake of their art. Virtually all dreams on film restructure sleep patterns to conform to a more artistic representation of the dream state. Even films that include "scientific" sleep labs (such as *Dreamscape*, *A Nightmare on Elm Street*, and *The Cell* [2000]) manipulate facts to depict sane people unable to distinguish dreams from reality.

Specifically, films mistakenly portray REM mentation during NREM manifestation. Sleepers will toss, turn, murmur, or shout (indicating NREM) yet have richly symbolic dreams, with vivid images contained with a definite story structure (indicating REM). Would reporter and Los Angeles Lakers fan Irwin Fletcher (Chevy Chase) in *Fletch* (1985) actually smile and roll his head during a wish fulfillment dream in which he plays basketball with his beloved team? Could Anakin Skywalker (Hayden Christensen) repeatedly shout "No" during his nightmares in *Star Wars: Episode II — Attack of the Clones*? While more interesting for the audience, this inconsistency is scientifically impossible, except in cases of severe sleep disturbances such as chronic insomnia (sleeping too little), hypersomnia (sleeping too much, as in narcolepsy) and parasomnia (sleeping in disrupted patterns, as in sleepwalking), all discussed further in Chapter 4.

Despite frequency, longevity, and apparent existence throughout all species for all time, our knowledge of dream functioning remains limited; research has provided insights into physiology, yet the psychological functions of dreaming — like dream interpretation — remain elusive, more closely resembling a self-expressive exploration of internal truth (art) than a reliable method for deciphering external facts (science). Scientific studies — measurable, repeatable, and falsifiable — have determined that humans and animals reap the physiological benefits of dream-related sleep cycles that include REM sleep and NREM sleep, yet the psychological benefits of dreaming remain shrouded in mystery.

Chapter 3

Dream Structure

In *Terminator 2: Judgment Day* (1991), Sarah Conner (Linda Hamilton) is sought by the T-1000 (the deadliest Terminator of them all), the police, government officials, and an angry group of doctors from the mental hospital from which she escaped, yet still manages to relax on cue. Seconds after sitting at a picnic table, she places her head down on the rotting wood and falls into a deep sleep in which she dreams of the impending nuclear holocaust. The dream structure is not scattered thoughts as in NREM sleep, but a complete story with a beginning, middle, and ending, indicating REM mentation. Despite the filmed depiction of speed sleepers such as Sarah Conner, who conveniently bypass the intermediate stages of sleep and transform instantly from a waking state to REM sleep, in real life the transition is slightly more complicated.

Dreams produced during NREM sleep often contain repetitive and worrisome images. Studies reveal that NREM dreams do not contain the irrational and impossible qualities of REM dreams; they portray obsessive qualities such as worrying and perseverating, i.e., persevering in a nonproductive repetitive thought-loop. "It is this rutlike quality of NREM dreams that leads us to describe them as illogical, or unrealistic, or unproductive. It is not that the laws of logic or physics are standardly violated in NREM dreams, as they are sometimes in REM dreams" (Flanagan, 2000, 141). Before a sleeper can access the bizarre psychotic imagery of REM mentation, he or she must wade through the mundane neurotic mental content associated with NREM sleep.

The activation-synthesis model of dreaming, proposed in 1977 by Robert McCarley and J. Allan Hobson of Harvard Medical School, refutes Freudian and Jungian theories of storylike dreams with a dramatic structure. They describe a purely physiological model of dreaming in which REM sleep initiates random electrical signals to the higher mental centers of the forebrain, thus creating fanciful but totally meaningless images from the lack of external stimuli. According to this theory, the brain automatically organizes these incoming groups of signals into a story that, if remembered, we try to rationalize and analyze upon awakening.

The Form and Content of Dreams

Of little interest to the sleeper, the psychoanalyst, or the movie-going public, NREM mentation and the activation-synthesis model are not the stuff film dreams are made of. Freud's psychological view that explains dreamed images as repressed instinctual urges and unfulfilled desires—all carefully disguised through dream symbols—translates far better on the big screen than a purely physiological approach. This view lends itself especially well to film because Freud says the form and content of dreams are intimately related. "The form of the dream or of dreaming is employed with astonishing frequency to represent the concealed content" (Freud, 1994, 222).

Therefore, a dream contained within the framework of a jog through the park symbolizes the dreamer is attempting to run away from his problem (*Keeping the Faith* [1999]). Likewise, in *The Princess Bride* (1987) based on William Goldman's 1973 novel of the same name, the superficial spell of beauty and happiness is broken in a fairy tale dream (contained within a bedtime story) when a filthy peasant shouts vile obscenities at the future queen to portray the ugly truth beneath the surface, the hideous betrayal that Buttercup (Robin Wright) feels upon marrying a prince she despises:

> Your true love lives and you marry another. True love saved her in the fire swamp and she treated it like garbage. And that's what she is—the queen of refuse. So bow down to her if you want, bow to her, bow to the queen of slime, the queen of filth, the queen of putrescence. Boo! Boo! Rubbish! Filth! Slime! Muck! Boo! Boo! Boo!

Although the DVD scene selections give the title "Booing the Queen" to this particular scene, a more accurate title for the dream sequence would be "Buttercup Unconsciously Booing Herself." The ancient booer in the dream represents a lifetime of self-hate as Buttercup ages from a lovely young woman into a miserable old hag. The layers of framework surrounding the dream may soften the blow for viewers unaccustomed to examining their own inner slime, filth, and putrescence.

Not surprisingly, Freud cites several examples of repressed sexuality revealed through the form of a dream. He describes a woman whose "hazy and confused" dream recall about an expectant baby indicates confusion

In *The Princess Bride*, a loving grandfather (Peter Falk) reads a fairy tale to his sick grandson (Fred Savage), thus creating a dream within a story within a dream, a framework that helps distance the dream sequence in both form and content as long ago and far away (20th Century–Fox, 1987).

about the father of her child, and a young man who dreams of visiting a hotel but has "gaps" in his memory about what he did when he mistakenly enters a room in which two young women are undressing. Freud theorizes that the gaps in his patient's memory represent "genital apertures of the women" (Freud, 1994, 222). He also speculates that dreams completely "wiped clean" from memory may well relate to an anal fixation.

Freud also writes about how the form of sleep relates to the dream. "In other dreams in which the inability to do something occurs, not merely as a situation, but also as a sensation, the same contradiction is more emphatically expressed by the sensation of inhibited movement, or a will to which a counter-will is opposed.... This very motor paralysis during sleep is one of the fundamental conditions of the psychic process which functions during dreaming" (227). He concludes that this physical and emotional inhibition produces anxiety dreams.

The many dreams contained within *In Dreams* (1998) rely on this Freudian connection between form and content. Claire Cooper (Annette Bening) has clairvoyant dreams sent to her telepathically by serial killer Vivian Thompson (Robert Downey, Jr.). Each dream reveals more about Vivian, but also leaves out a crucial piece of information necessary for

Claire to make sense of the dreams. "I need an interpreter for whatever the hell it is I dream," she laments. Her dreams are filled with these provocative gaps and haziness. She dreams of kissing Vivian gently, then violently. She obsesses about him during her waking and dreaming hours; when Claire is eventually locked up in a psychiatric hospital, she sleeps in the same room where he was once incarcerated, and of course, dreams of him there. Using blatant and frequent symbolism, Vivian, who lives in an apple cider factory, transmits images of apples through dreams, visions, and computer screens in his efforts to tempt and seduce Claire. At the same time repulsed and attracted, terrified and unafraid, Claire is a Freudian dream come true: In form and content, her dreams depict the aggressive, violent, and sexual urges secretly repressed by Claire and openly expressed by Vivian.

Dreams as Stories

Jung also provides insights into the storylike form of dreams usually associated with REM sleep. Differing in psychic structure from other types of thought, these dreams are inherently interesting because of their uniqueness. Jung writes in *Dreams* (1974):

> So far as we can judge from their form and meaning, they [dreams] do not show the continuity of development typical of conscious contents. They do not appear, as a rule, to be integral components of our conscious psychic life, but seem rather to be extraneous, apparently accidental occurrences. The reason for this exceptional position of dreams lies in their peculiar mode of origin: they do not arise, like other conscious contents, from any clearly discernible, logical and emotional continuity of experience, but are remnants of a peculiar psychic activity taking place during sleep [28].

Although NREM dreams take the predictable form of a nagging conscience or endless thought loop, REM dreams often resemble a predictable story in form, with decidedly unpredictable content based on this psychic activity.

Jung divides this dramatic structure of the dream narrative into four parts. Beginning with *exposition*, the dream provides a statement of place and description of protagonists, indicating the scene of the action, the characters involved, and the initial situation of the dreamer. The second part, *development*, reveals complications to the original situation and growing feelings of tension. The third part of a dream brings the *culmination* where something decisive happens or a change initiates a new situation.

Serial killer (and apple cider factory dweller) Vivian Thompson (Robert Downey, Jr.) telepathically transmits dreams with red apples to Claire Cooper (Annette Bening) in the thriller *In Dreams* (DreamWorks Pictures, 1998). Photograph by Francois Duhamel.

The fourth part is the *solution* or *result*, the final solution sought by the dreamer and produced by the dreamwork (Jung, 1974, 80–81).

Wild Strawberries, Ingmar Bergman's 1957 exploration of fantasy, memories, dreams, and nightmares, begins with Dr. Isak Borg (Swedish actor and director Victor Sjostrom), a seventy-eight-year-old professor of medicine and a reclusive widower, introducing himself through a voiceover to the audience the day before he receives an honorary degree for fifty years as a doctor. This scene cuts to the opening credits and is followed by a dream sequence in which Dr. Borg reveals the dream he had that night in which he wanders through a strange town.

Presented as a flashback and a dream, his remembrance of the dream introduces the sequence, then switches to a real-time representation of the dream from which he is shown awakening the next morning. The dream tells a symbolic story that will be replayed throughout the film through dreams, flashbacks, and new experiences. Although unrealistically depicted in black and white (due to technical limitations at the time the Swedish film was made), the dream otherwise stays true to the science of the day, specifically Jung's theory of dramatic structure.

During the dream's exposition, Dr. Borg establishes that he has lost his way on his morning walk. He wanders aimlessly through the empty streets, looking at the ruined buildings for a familiar landmark. The dream's development begins with Dr. Borg seeing a large clock with no hands above a deserted eye doctor's office. As he notices the clock, a heart-beat begins to pulse in the background. He looks at his own pocket watch and confirms that it, too, has no hands. The doctor is noticeably shaken by this discovery and the heartbeats stop as he walks in another direction.

Culmination in the dream surrounds the sudden appearance of a man with his back to Dr. Borg. He approaches the man, touching his shoulder to turn him around. He is frightened to see that the man is a stuffed dummy that immediately crumples to the ground and bleeds upon being touched by the doctor. The solution is announced by bells chiming and the arrival of a driverless carriage drawn by two horses. The carriage carries a casket, which is forcefully knocked to the ground when a wheel of the carriage noisily crashes into a lamppost. The casket opens and a limp hand extends outward. Dr. Borg walks closer for a better look and the hand grabs him. As the body emerges from the casket, the dead — yet undead — victim is revealed as himself. He stares into his own lifeless face with terror.

The aging professor does not need a psychoanalyst to convey the meaning of the dream. The next day, Dr. Borg tries to tell his daughter-in-law Marianne (Ingrid Thulin) about the dream, but she says she is not interested. Later after another series of disturbing dreams, he insists on sharing his experience with her.

"Recently, I've had the most weird dreams, as if I must tell myself something I won't listen to when I'm awake," he tells her.

"What's that?" she asks.

"That I'm dead. Although I'm alive."

Dr. Borg understands the meaning of his dream, i.e., he follows the dramatic structure of the dream narrative, but in keeping with the Jungian concept of a dream series having more importance than a single dream, he does not fully realize the personal significance of these dreams until he endures several related nightmares that review his family history, love life, and career choice. He tells Marianne: "I dozed off, but was haunted by vivid and humiliating dreams. There was something overpowering in these dreamed images that bored relentlessly into my mind."

Jung suggests in *Dreams* (1974) that this overpowering element of dreams may be their elusive meanings, which generally lie just beyond our reach. Fantastic ideas linked together in an illogical sequence contrasts sharply with the normal logical flow of ideas inherent in the conscious mental processes. Because of this illogical flow, dreams are often considered meaningless. "But before pronouncing this verdict we should remember that the dream and its content is something that we do not understand. With such a verdict, therefore, we would merely be projecting our own lack of understanding upon the object. But that would not prevent dreams from having an inherent meaning of their own" (24). It is precisely this inherent meaning that eludes Dr. Borg, at least until the end of the film.

Dream Fragments

Although this particular *Wild Strawberries* dream sequence uses only five minutes of screen time, an actual REM dream lasts about twenty minutes during a ninety-minute cycle. Freud's theory of condensation works hard here; dream elements are selected by directors to develop the story within the dream as well as the overall story of the film, all within an approximately two-hour time frame. In sci-fi thrillers such as *Twelve Monkeys* (1995) and *Sleepy Hollow* (1999), dreams are presented throughout the film in brief fragments with each fragment revealing another piece of the puzzle and heightening the tension. Dramas such as *Ordinary People* (1980) also may begin with a partial dream, establishing a tone, looking into someone's psyche, and leaving the audience with an important mystery to solve.

Dream fragments that appear later in films such as *Kindergarten Cop* (1990) can serve one specific purpose — in this case a warning — and longer dreams near the end of films such as *Cat People* (1982) help propel the action towards an inevitable conclusion. In comedies such as *National Lampoon's European Vacation* (1985), dreams are complete stories lasting several minutes with little direct relevance to the plot of the story, designed simply to produce additional comic relief based on the frailties of the dreamer. Filmed dream sequences generally go beyond Freud's theory of a form-content relationship and Jung's concept of a storylike structure, linking the dream's form, content, placement, style, importance, and interpretation with its overall purpose within the film.

In *City Edition* (1980), a short black-and-white experimental film by Emmy Award-winning documentary filmmaker and installation artist Alan Berliner, a newspaper printing press starts the film, which consists entirely of a montage of "found footage" representing news items from around the world gathered from a variety of sources. Connected either visually, aurally, or thematically, these images include an overall incoherent assortment of marches, executions, races, sporting events, and celebrity footage. At the end of the film, a man wakes and turns off his alarm clock, indicating the rush of images was only a dream. These images, like those in the daily newspaper tossed carelessly into the trash, are only momentarily meaningful.

In the short film *City Edition* (1980), a newspaper with random juxtapositions and implausible connections is tossed into the trash just like the daily residue of our dreams is forgotten upon awakening. Film still courtesy of Alan Berliner.

Berliner, whose personal documentaries include *Nobody's Business* (1996) and *The Sweetest Sound* (2001), says the form of the man's dream is crucial to its content: The purpose of showing the images as dream is to make sense of non-sense.

> The use of the dream sequence in *City Edition* is a way of linking the overwhelming array of information — sounds, images and ideas, what we usually refer to as "information overload" — that is inextricably woven into the experience of modern urban existence, with the terribly unstructured place called the unconscious — the Dodge City of the mind, the storehouse of images, feelings, hopes and wishes, the unkempt repository of every memory, every detail of experience we didn't even know (or remember) we remembered, a factory where random juxtapositions and implausible connections are and can be manufactured each and every day or in the case of sleep, every night.[6]

A dramatic structure — even a meandering one — rationalized and analyzed upon awakening (or leaving the theater) helps us automatically organize incoming groups of signals into our brains during a dreamlike state. Making sense out of non-sense, however, becomes more complex when we are deprived of sleep, and therefore, of REM mentation.

Chapter 4

Sleep Deprivation

Although the alien crime fighters in *Men in Black* (1997) can function on a thirty-seven-hour day, most of us cannot. We need our eight or so hours of sleep each night of a twenty-four-hour day in order to stay physically fit and mentally alert. Studies on sleep deprivation have shown that laboratory animals deprived of REM sleep for extended periods will sicken and die. Under controlled circumstances, human test subjects have gone without sleep for eleven days, but obviously have not risked death to participate in a case study. In addition to predictable effects such as stomach upset, increased sensitivity to pain, tiredness, and irritability, severe sleep deprivation can cause hypnagogic experiences, i.e., vivid hallucinations during the transition from waking to sleeping.

Although we still lack a definitive explanation for human sleep patterns, the adaptive theory maintains that specieswide sleep patterns developed as a way of adapting to the environment. Accordingly, grazing animals sleep relatively few hours a day in short bursts as a response to the necessity of constant alertness for predators. In contrast, animals with few natural enemies, such as gorillas, sleep up to fifteen hours per day. Adaptive theory hypothesizes that human sleep patterns developed after the species began living in caves, which offered protection from nighttime predators (Lewis, 1995).

Sleep Patterns

Human sleep patterns also change over the course of a lifetime. Recent studies suggest that near-term fetuses spend about sixty to eighty percent of their sleep time in REM sleep; babies sleep about half the time in REM sleep; and most adults spend about twenty-five percent (or about two hours a night) in REM sleep. This percentage continues to lower as we age, so that in our later years of life, we have relatively little REM sleep — only fifteen to twenty percent of the time asleep (Dement and Vaughan, 1999). In *Spellbound* (1945), when the aging psychiatrist Dr. Alex Brulov (Michael Chekhov, nephew of playwright Anton) says, "When you're old, you don't need to sleep so much," he is quoting science of his time that is still believed today.

A constant war exists between waking consciousness and sleep debt. "Sleep dept is always driving the brain toward sleep, while stimulation from the biological clock and the environment is promoting wakefulness" (Dement and Vaughan, 1999, 230). We tend to be poor judges of our sleepiness because the alertness-sleepiness continuum is a complex function only moderately affected by outside stimulants such as too much coffee, a heavy workload, or depression. Our likelihood of falling asleep actually depends upon the combination of two opposing forces: sleep load minus level of alerting. "We may be so excited or stressed by external stimulation that we don't perceive a huge sleep dept" (Dement and Vaughan, 1999, 65).

One soldier in this war between waking consciousness and sleep debt is widower Sam Baldwin (Tom Hanks) in *Sleepless in Seattle* (1993). A depressed insomniac who channels all his energy into work, Sam is a poor judge of his own sleepiness and expresses surprise when his son dubs him "Sleepless in Seattle" during a call-in radio talk show. Conversely, his son has no trouble falling asleep, but suffers from nightmares that awaken him. A huge sleep dept is accruing between the two Baldwin men.

This also is the case in the action comedy *Into the Night* (1985). Chronic insomniac Ed Okin (Jeff Goldblum) has an unfaithful wife and a dead-end job as an aerospace engineer. On an aimless late-night drive to the airport, he picks up Diana (Michelle Pfeiffer), a beautiful international jewel smuggler being chased by various deadly factions. Although Ed claims he has not had a full night's sleep since "the summer of 1980," he manages to drive Diana around Los Angeles for nearly forty-eight hours. Severely sleep-deprived Ed dozes at his desk and at board meetings, yet amazingly can stay wide awake while driving. Apparently he is so excited or stressed by the external stimulation of Pfeiffer's provocatively dressed and decidedly dangerous character that he does not perceive a huge sleep debt and therefore manages to stay awake.

Contrary to scientific findings regarding sleep deprivation, he exhibits no signs of stomach upset (eats a rich ice cream sundae and drinks coffee at an all-night diner), increased sensitivity to pain (gets roughed up repeatedly by professional thugs and emerges without a scratch or bruise), confusion (navigates his way all around Los Angeles), irritability (calmly endures lies, insults, a profane Elvis impersonator, high-speed car chases, and a hotel room full of dead bodies), or hypnagogic experiences. Ed is tired though, and complains about it incessantly.

In fact, Ed's sleep deprivation provides an improbable shield against unexpected inconveniences like a gun stuffed in his mouth. He tells Diana, "I'm too tired for all this. I don't need any more shit in my life right now." However, the audience knows that going into the night is exactly what he needs. Lack of sleep — a result of his personal and professional crises — has produced a desperate man with nothing left to lose. Helping Diana in her life-and-death struggle provides the spiritual fulfillment, mental stimulation, and physical activity previously missing from his daily existence. In the end, Ed finds a cure for his insomnia, and more importantly, finds meaning in his life.

On the other hand, insomniac Will Dormer (Al Pacino), a Los Angeles police detective sent to solve a homicide in Nightmute, Alaska, in the thriller *Insomnia* (2002), exhibits the classic symptoms of sleep deprivation. He has increased sensitivity to pain and noise, confusion (even about his own guilt and innocence), increasing irritability, and hypnagogic experiences where he imagines scenes from the murder case. Dormer once said: "A good cop can't sleep because he's missing a piece of the puzzle, and a bad cop can't sleep because his conscience won't let him." These words come back to haunt him as he struggles with his personal and professional values in a land where the sun never sets. By the end of the film, his mental and emotional state has deteriorated almost completely.

Scientific studies show that depriving people of REM sleep will not make them mentally ill, but outward appearances may seem otherwise. In the low-budget thriller *The Blair Witch Project* (1999), reality blurs with illusion in every aspect of the film, including depriving the actors/characters of sleep. During filming, directors Daniel Myrick and Eduardo Sanchez transformed the tranquil beauty of Maryland's Seneca Creek State Park into the haunted Black Hills Forest, the site where three student filmmakers (played by Heather Donahue, Michael Williams, and Joshua Leonard) mysteriously disappear during filming of a documentary about the mythical Blair Witch. Shot on video and 16mm film, in color and black and white, the feature is a hybrid of looks created by method filmmaking.

The unsuspecting actors did not know what awaited them as they wandered through the woods, deprived of sleep, proper nourishment, and knowledge of the production team's plans, which included nightly harassments, haunted images, and a bloody discovery wrapped in flannel. Sanchez says although the production team spent countless hours walking through the woods before the shoot, the tedious scouting was well worth it. Their in-depth knowledge of the woods was crucial for the nightly

The production team at Haxan Films (from left: Dan Myrick [co-director, co-writer], Robin Cowie [producer], Gregg Hale [producer], Mike Monello [co-producer], Eduardo Sanchez [co-director, co-writer]) deprived their actors of sleep and food to get more realistic performances in *The Blair Witch Project.* (Artisan Entertainment, 1999). Photograph by Julie Ann Smith.

hauntings staged by the production team. "My favorite part was waking up the actors at 3:00 a.m. and scaring them," Sanchez says (Halpern, 1999, D-2). To facilitate these supposed encounters between the filmmakers and the Blair Witch, the production team moved quietly through the woods—sometimes a mile or more in the dark — using red-lens headlamps. Filming just before Halloween added to the ambience.

According to Ben Rock, production designer for *The Blair Witch Project*, the actors are not doing much acting by the end of the film — their terror is real.

> The actors experienced a mixture of food and sleep deprivation: At the beginning they could have what they wanted to eat, but by the end of the eight-day shoot, we gave each of them a power bar and a glass of water for the day. We made them walk through the woods all day with heavy packs of junk on their backs, and we were disturbing them every night with loud noises... All of us have been deprived of sleep sometimes and after awhile, you hallucinate. It takes all your energy just to stand up and function. Sleep deprivation wears you down as a person, and these actors got worn down.[7]

Rock notes that in order to harass the actors each night, the production team was sleep deprived as well. Although certainly not the primary goal of the filmmakers, *The Blair Witch Project* provides one of the truest representations of sleep deprivation ever filmed.

Sleep Disorders

Besides chronic insomnia (whether caused by physical ailments, psychological trauma, or filmmakers intent on realism), any one of about eighty sleep disorders can get in the way of a good night's rest. Hypersomnia (sleeping too much, as in narcolepsy) is caused by a malfunction in the brain that triggers sleep inappropriately. Though incurable, narcolepsy is treatable with stimulants that counter patients' daytime sleepiness. "Narcolepsy is a disease in which the daily periods of internal clock-dependent alerting appear to be missing. The physician, then, is using drugs to replace this important internal function" (Dement and Vaughan, 1999, 206).

Because filmmakers usually want to contrast the dream life with the waking life (except when they plan the opposite [see Chapter 16]), a depiction of too much sleeping and dreaming can lose its ability to intrigue an audience. In *The Cell* (2000), for example, the comatose killer remains trapped in a perpetual dreamland. In order to shock the viewer with the malevolence of his dreams, we also see the benevolent imaginings of a dream-linking therapist and the real world, as created within this film. In *Sleepy Hollow* (1999), reluctant hero Ichabod Crane (Johnny Depp) has three bright, colorful dreams that contrast the dark, drab oppressive atmosphere of Sleepy Hollow. Resembling a hypersomniac, he falls asleep frequently and easily with instant REM mentation, which proves a helpful escape from the dismal situation in which he finds himself.

Though narcoleptics on film are in short supply, sleepwalkers—one manifestation of parasomnia, or disrupted sleep patterns—remain a popular image. People afflicted with sleepwalking and night terrors will rise out of an apparent deep sleep and act as if they are awake; they typically do not respond to other people and have no memory of the incident the next day. Unlike REM behavior disorder, however, people are not dreaming when they sleepwalk and are not having nightmares during these night terrors (Dement and Vaughan, 1999, 211). The seemingly supernatural aspect of walking in one's sleep while in an altered state of consciousness makes sleepwalkers a perfect image for horror films. In *Bram Stoker's Dracula* (1992), the blood-lusting Count (Gary Oldman) has the ability to lure

his sleeping victim outside to the garden where he drinks her blood and brutally rapes her. She has no memory of the repeated attacks, and therefore can offer no assistance to Dr. Van Helsing and his crew of angry vampire hunters. When Dracula eventually comes after his primary target, Mina Murray (Winona Ryder), his presence awakens the sleeping beauty, and his gaze transfixes her.

As the legend goes, vampires—creatures of the night—sneak up on sleeping victims (usually helpless women) and sink their teeth into the neck, draining just enough blood to keep the victims alive. Legend also gives the vampires the ability to transform into non-human forms in order in make a stealthy entrance (e.g., green mist under the door) or a hasty pre-dawn exit (e.g., bat from the window). Their victims sleepwalk, sleeptalk, and otherwise endure a continued state of altered consciousness which is neither fully awake, fully asleep, fully alive, nor fully dead. Despite the blood and violence, Francis Ford Coppola insists that his film presents more romance than horror. "Blood was used as a symbol of passion, and Dracula is a very passionate character. The film remains faithful to Bram Stoker's original book, which is an erotic nightmare whose message is that love is stronger than death" (Halpern, 1992, 4).

The classic animated example of sleepwalking is, of course, *Sleeping Beauty* (1959), in which Princess Aurora follows a hypnotic green mist down the hall and up the stairs to the attic where she encounters a spinning wheel with a nasty spindle. After she pricks her finger on the spindle as ordained at birth by the evil fairy Maleficent, Princess Aurora falls into a deathlike sleep that affects everything in the kingdom ... except her beauty.

Dreaming and Driving

Another popular way to represent sleep deprivation on film is to show drivers falling asleep at the wheel of a car. Brought on by the monotony of driving and accumulated sleep debt, and compounded by darkness, falling asleep while driving is decidedly unfunny, though often depicted humorously on film. "Driving drowsy has exactly the same risk and tragic consequences as driving drunk.... Often people do not know they are sleep deprived and are surprised when a strong wave of drowsiness strikes while

Opposite: Ichabod Crane (Johnny Depp) should have packed smelling salts, coffee, and sugary sweets in his luggage. The squeamish inspector faints, sleeps, and dreams throughout his entire visit to *Sleepy Hollow*. (Paramount Pictures and Mandalay Pictures LLC, 1999). Photograph by Clive Coote.

they are asleep behind the wheel" (Dement and Vaughan, 1999, 393). According to a recent survey by the National Sleep Foundation, twenty-three percent of the people surveyed admitted falling asleep while driving in the past year. "With this in mind, it should be no surprise that sleep deprivation plays a major role in most accidents labeled 'cause unknown,' or that an estimated 24,000 people die each year in accidents caused directly or in part by falling asleep at the wheel" (Dement and Vaughan, 1999, 4).

While sleep deprivation plays a major role in many tragic car accidents, falling asleep at the wheel plays a minor role in many comedy films. In *National Lampoon's Vacation* (1983), the bumbling Clark W. Griswold (Chevy Chase) drives his family in a newly purchased Wagon Queen Family Truckster ("You think you hate it now, but wait till you drive it") on a road trip from Chicago to California's mythical Wally World. On their first night of driving, his wife, Ellen, (Beverly D'Angelo) suggests they get off the road as soon as possible. "You're tired... Let's just find a motel. I don't want you dozing off." Clark replies: "I'm not tired. Are you kidding? I could go another hundred miles."

The next scene shows close-ups of the two sleeping children in the backseat, Ellen resting peacefully and Clark, open-mouthed and snoring at the wheel as the Truckster careens along the highway and veers off an exit ramp. Clark sleeps through several high-speed near-accidents and only awakens when Ellen mumbles to "turn off the TV and come to bed." He wakes up enough to realize the danger and slams on the brakes. The chances of a sleepy but stubborn father falling asleep while driving on a road trip are high. The chances of a family surviving an asleep-at-the-wheel driver without a scratch (as the Griswolds did) are significantly lower.

Lloyd Christmas (Jim Carrey) proves even dumber than Clark W. Griswold in 1994's *Dumb and Dumber*, Peter Farrelly's directorial debut. Driving across the country in a van altered to look like a sheep dog, Lloyd manages to encounter the dangers of falling asleep at the wheel and narrowly avoid a deadly collision without even technically falling asleep. Lloyd enjoys a lengthy fantasy sequence (daydream) — during which his eyes are wide open — while precariously weaving along the interstate. In *Dreams and Symbols*, Lucien Morgan gives a possible explanation for this type of occurrence: "Sleep deprivation means dream deprivation, and it is this that can bring about severe disorientation, even hallucinations, because the dreams that are being denied in the normal way are taking place during the waking state" (1996, 17).

Similarly, the childlike Pee-wee Herman (Paul Reubens) is much safer riding his bicycle than driving a car in *Pee-wee's Big Adventure* (1985).

While an escaped convict sleeps in the passenger seat of a stolen car, Pee-wee rubs his sleepy eyes, but remains awake as he barely maneuvers the treacherous mountain curves during the dark of night. In a surrealistic scene resembling a dream sequence, the car plunges off a cliff and falls down in slow motion as the two men scream, then lands safely on the ground in a jungle-like atmosphere with wild beasts. When it comes to intelligence, Lloyd and Pee-wee are figuratively asleep at the wheel.

In a dramatic film where every scene resembles a dream sequence, Federico Fellini's *8½* (1963) provides an ironic twist to the asleep-at-the-wheel image. While visiting a health spa to relax, revered Italian director Guido (Marcello Mastroianni) dreams of being trapped inside an immobile car (perhaps a symbol for his sleep-immobilized body) filled with suffocating smoke. Although the aforementioned drivers are driving in a deadly dreamlike state, Guido dreams of a deadly drive. Artistically, being asleep at the wheel is a clever analogy for empty-headedness, and being dead in the car a surreal symbol of one who is lost in life, but falling asleep while driving is easily explained by hard, serious scientific facts associated with sleep deprivation.

Chapter 5

Dreams Under the Influence

When obsessive college professor Dr. Eddie Jessup (William Hurt) ingests hallucinogenic mushrooms and jumps naked into an isolation tank in the film *Altered States* (1980), we easily believe the resulting series of shocking dreams and frightening visions are intensified because of his drug use. In his quest to return to the primordial essence of man, Jessup experiences various altered states of consciousness accompanied by dreams with illogical images, displaced illusions, and abrupt scene shifts that reflect the heightened sensitivity usually associated with mood-elevating drugs. However, in filmed dream sequences, troubled insomniacs who consume tranquilizing drugs or alcohol before going to sleep also produce vivid dreams that exceed what most of us would consider "normal." In contrast to scientific findings, movie dreams under the influence of any drug are presented as somehow more insightful and symbolic because of this added dimension.

Although prevalent in films today, this myth of dreams experienced under the influence is nothing new. In 1909, Gustavus Hindman Miller defined three types of dreams in *A Dictionary of Dreams*: subjective, spiritual and physical. Subjective dreams possess a symbolic element of warning and prophecy. Spiritual dreams are brought about by the higher self penetrating the soul realm and reflecting upon the waking mind. Physical dreams are less important, he writes, and are usually superinduced by the anxious waking mind, possessing no prophetic significance. "Dreams induced by opiates, fevers, mesmerism and ill health come under this class.... Such dreams reflect only the present condition of the body and mind of the dreamer; but as the past and present enter into shaping the future, the reflection thus left on the waking mind should not go by unheeded" (Miller, 1992, 20–21). Films depict subjective and spiritual dreams, often in conjunction with the elements of what Miller would call a physical dream.

College professor Eddie Jessup (William Hurt) learns that ingesting hallucinogenic mushrooms has some uncomfortable side effects in *Altered States* (Warner Bros., 1980).

Sleeping Potions

As long as people have had insomnia, doctors have been prescribing sleeping potions containing alcohol, opium, or other tranquilizers. Introduced in 1869, the first synthetic sleeping potion was chloral hydrate, which along with similar drugs was chemically classified as bromide salts or bromides. Sleep expert William C. Dement writes: "These medications were no great improvement over existing ones because they also could be addictive, and an overdose could kill…. It wasn't until 1903 that barbital was developed, which gave rise to a large class of sleep-inducing compounds called barbiturates. Although developed for anesthesia, barbiturates were widely prescribed as sleeping pills well into the 1970s" (Dement and Vaughan, 1999, 160). In low doses, barbiturates release inhibitions; in high doses, they calm the central nervous system, inducing deep unconsciousness.

Barbiturate dependency and overdose led to the introduction of other drugs such as Librium and Valium in the 1970s that treat anxiety by relaxing muscles and inducing sleep. In 1992, the United States approved a new sleep medication, Ambien, which works as a short-term hypnotic with less addictive qualities and higher selectivity in nerve cell interaction. These various medications "all work through the same process. They activate the brain's governor, a brake that holds back nerve activity and keeps the nervous system from burning itself out" (Dement and Vaughan, 1999, 162).

The idea that intoxicants such as drugs and alcohol enhance the creative process of the conscious (i.e., fully awake) mind remains controversial. However, the unconscious (i.e., dreaming or in a dream-like state of) mind naturally produces seemingly psychotic images and ideas without the aid of intoxicants, which may actually interfere with the dreaming process. According to studies cited in James R. Lewis' *The Dream Encyclopedia* (1995), REM sleep, and therefore dreams, decrease under the influence of drugs designed to help patients sleep.

> Studies of alcohol and dreams, for example, indicate the quantity of REM sleep decreases and Stage 4 (deep) sleep increases with excessive alcohol consumption, creating the impression that one has slept more deeply and more soundly under the influence of alcohol. REM sleep also decreases under the influence of barbiturates, drugs that in the past were regularly prescribed to help stressed-out patients sleep and relax. As with many other drugs, REM sleep initially decreases under the influence of barbiturates, but later returns to a normal level if the drug is used regularly [Lewis, 1995, 77].

He notes, however, that withdrawal is difficult and regular users experience vivid dreams and nightmares when they attempt to stop abusing their drugs of choice.

Studies show that alcohol alone proves a poor sleeping potion. "Alcohol may not be a potent sedative by itself, but it becomes very sedating when paired with sleep debt. It is tempting to speculate that all sedatives, particularly sleeping pills, interact with sleep debt" (Dement and Vaughan, 1999, 68). If a sedative calms the senses in order to facilitate sleep in which nearly all sensory input ceases, then it cannot simultaneously stimulate those same senses to produce unusually exotic dreams.

The most famous cinematic sleeping potion was delivered in an apple by the evil queen to Snow White in the animated Walt Disney classic *Snow White and the Seven Dwarfs* (1937). In the dungeon of her castle, the jealous queen conjures up a disguise as an old peddler woman and prepares a magic sleeping potion in a bubbling vat. "The poisoned apple. Sleeping Death. Dip the apple in the brew. Let the sleeping death seep through," she chants. "When she breaks the tender peel to taste the apple in my hand, her breath will still, her blood congeal, then I'll be fairest in the land." The naive Snow White, hiding at the home of the seven dwarfs, succumbs to an Eve-like temptation of the apple offered by the queen in her disguise. "One bite and all your dreams will come true," she promises Snow White. Later, after falling into the sleeping death, Snow White comes back to life because the prince unknowingly has the antidote she needs: "The victim of the sleeping death can be revived only by love's first kiss." Other films, including *The Company of Wolves* (1984), *Living in Oblivion* (1994), *In Dreams* (1998), and *End of Days* (1999) also combine apples, dreams, magic, and sex.

Myth and Art

Much of the fascination surrounding dreams and drugs involves mythology and artistic representation, i.e., non-scientific explorations of altered states of mind. Besides, down-and-out heroes with a temporary reliance on drugs or alcohol who receive profound dream messages from their unconscious mind and bravely act upon them make for sympathetic characters. In *End of Days*, Christine York (Robin Tunney) consumes the tranquilizer Xanax like candy, yet has suffered her entire life from vivid nightmares of having sex with Satan. Her protector, a suici-

Don't let his muscles and guns fool you. Suicidal security specialist Jericho (Arnold Schwarzenegger) is weakened by his chemical dependency and visions in *End of Days* (Universal Pictures and Beacon Pictures, 1999). Photograph by Zade Rosenthal.

Satan (Gabriel Byrne, right) tempts Jericho (Arnold Schwarzenegger) with a vision in which his murdered family is alive again in *End of Days* (Universal Pictures and Beacon Pictures, 1999). Photograph by Zade Rosenthal.

dal security specialist named Jericho (Arnold Schwarzenegger), is a recovering alcoholic who experiences several visions blamed on alcohol. In fact, the tongueless man who speaks, the creature-infested apple, and the reenactment of his family's murder by vengeful thugs all arise from supernatural causes brought about by Satan (Gabriel Byrne) rather than alcohol consumption. Yet Jericho's personal loss and chemical dependency make him seem vulnerable despite his magnificent muscles and non-stop firepower.

In *Dreamscape* (1984), the president of the United States (Eddie Albert) wields a different kind of power — a power weakened by his nightmares of disfigured children that reveal his increasing doubts about nuclear arms. A sinister plot to assassinate the president in his sleep by using a psychotic dream-link almost proves successful. Luckily, while enduring a vivid nightmare onboard a train filled with angry mutants, he is contacted in the dream by psychic hero Alex Gardner (Dennis Quaid), who tells him to wake up to save his life. "I can't," the president sadly replies in the dream. "They gave me sedatives."

Similarly, Kevin Kline's arrogant Bottom becomes more lovable after being made into an ass by Puck's magic potion in *William Shakespeare's A*

Heavily sedated, the president (Eddie Albert, center) cannot awaken from his nightmare in which a dream assassin (David Patrick Kelly, left) tries to kill him and a dream-linking hero (Dennis Quaid) tries to save him in *Dreamscape* (20th Century–Fox, 1983).

Midsummer Night's Dream (1999). "I have had a most rare vision. I have had a dream past the wit of man to say what dream it was. Man is but an ass if he go about to expound this dream," he says upon awakening. Humbled by the experience and confused because of his drug-induced dream/reality, Bottom becomes more fallible, believable, and likeable. By literally becoming an ass, he figuratively becomes less of one. Just in case the dreams, drugs, ass references, or sexual innuendos in the story prove too much for those in an unaltered state of consciousness, Puck (Stanley Tucci) suggests: "If we shadows have offended think but this and all is mended. That you have but slumbered here while these visions did appear. And this weak and idle theme no more yielding but a dream." Dreams, however, can yield themes of enormous importance, relevance, and imagination.

Romantic Imaginations

Like Elizabethan playwright-poet William Shakespeare, Romantic poet Samuel Taylor Coleridge also combines mythology and artistry of dreams under the influence. However, he takes it one step further by blurring boundaries between the art and the artist. In an introductory note to his masterpiece "Kubla Khan," Coleridge says that one night during the summer of 1797, a tranquilizing anodyne (opium) enhanced his dreaming which led to the creation of the lyric poem, composed entirely of dreamlike imagery. The poem begins with the lines:

> In Xanadu did Kubla Khan
> A stately pleasure-dome decree:
> Where Alph, the sacred river, ran
> Through caverns measureless to man
> Down to a sunless sea.

The poem continues with illogical images (dancing rocks, dome in the air), displaced illusions (ancestral voices prophesying war!), and abrupt scene shifts (A damsel with a dulcimer / In a vision once I saw) as in a REM-state dream. Although sleep science refutes Coleridge's claim that drugs enhanced his dream, the poet anticipates his readers' willing suspension of disbelief in order for the myth to continue (Halpern, 2001, 19).

A similar circumstance occurs in Alfred Hitchcock's 1945 psychological thriller *Spellbound*. Suffering from amnesia, suspected of murdering a prominent psychiatrist, and exhibiting an irrational and highly debilitating fear of black lines on a white background, JB (Gregory Peck) finds Dr. Constance Peterson (Ingrid Bergman), who becomes his newfound friend, lover, and on-call psychoanalyst. Her former mentor, Dr. Alex Brulov (Michael Chekhov), provides sanctuary for the fleeing couple, plus free bromides at night, and dream analysis over breakfast.

The good doctor slips so many bromides into JB's glass of milk that the disturbed amnesiac immediately falls into a deep sleep from which three shoulder slaps are needed to rouse him. "Enough bromides to knock out three horses," Dr. Brulov says. JB (later revealed as medical doctor John Ballantine) awakens from his drugged slumber to relate his own detailed masterpiece, nearly as rich and poetic as the work of Coleridge. Seemingly unable to produce the dream on his own, the bromides— intended to relax his senses— instead manage to excite, elevate, and exaggerate his ability to express himself through the symbolic language of dreams.

Based on designs by Surrealist painter Salvador Dalí, JB's dream not only professes his love for Constance, but explains his amnesia, solves the murder, and eliminates his guilt complex from childhood that led to that pesky aversion to black lines. Still rich with symbolism and one of the most famous dreams on film, most of Dalí's actual dream sequence footage was cut from the final version of the film as too distracting. Exotic scenes of eyeballs on curtains being sliced with scissors, a faceless man who threatens a gambler, a giant winged creature pursuing Ballantine, and a distorted wheel dropped by the faceless man remain in the sequence.

The widespread myth of drug-enhanced dreaming cannot be attributed to the film's mid-twentieth century release date or the director (Hitchcock's *Marnie* [1964] also features a pill-popping dreamer). In addition to *Dreamscape* and *End of Days*, other recent films such as the suspense thrillers *Twelve Monkeys* (1995), *In Dreams* (1998), and *Shattered Image* (1998) feature heavily sedated characters under psychiatric care still tortured by nightmares.

Independent filmmaker Alan Berliner used a non-drug-enhanced dream sequence in his early experimental film, *City Edition* (1980). He says the psychological elements brought together in his montage of old news footage and later revealed as a dream, however, could have been achieved by other means besides a dream.

> Other devices to accomplish similar ends include cinematic representations of drug trips, drunken stupors, overwhelming human circumstances like starvation, sleep deprivation, near death experience, intense psychological/emotional stress or any other representation of altered states of consciousness, which allow/release the power of the mind to think outside of itself, to live outside of itself, to lose touch with reality — and in the best spirit of human ingenuity — to come up with its own solutions.[8]

Yet Berliner chose a dream sequence, instead of these other means (or combinations of means), because he says naturally occurring dreams are reassuring for the audience.

Combining the reassurance of a dream with the threat of the unknown effects of a drug proves irresistible to many filmmakers. However, whether found in film, poetry, or any form of art, the sedative-enhanced dream simply defies common sense. Although science dictates that sedatives sedate and stimulants stimulate, filmed dream sequences have their own unique logic. Regardless of what science says about alcohol, drugs, and dreaming, the idea of drug-enhanced dream states inspires readers and audiences to build an infinite "stately pleasure-dome" in their own romantic imaginations.

Chapter 6

Waking Up

In *Shattered Image* (1998), a young woman (Anne Parillaud) wakes up from her dream of being an assassin in New York to find herself a honeymooner in Jamaica until she wakes up from that dream to find herself an assassin in New York who dreamed herself a honeymooner in Jamaica. The confusing cycle of sleeping, dreaming, and awakening continues throughout the film until she finally wakes up in a hospital after a six-month coma and must sort out the dreams from the reality. The audience finds itself in the same predicament of sorting out the true meaning of her dreams. *Vanilla Sky* (2001) uses the same technique so we never know if the character is waking from a dream, or waking within a dream.

Freud theorizes that the mind produces an internal censor that disguises the true meaning of dreams in order to allow a good night's rest. Although current sleep scientists reject the theory of psychological dream composition as a sleep protector, they agree that physiological factors keep us asleep. In *The Dream Encyclopedia* (1995), James R. Lewis concludes that normal REM sleep immobility "is a biological mechanism for preventing us from awakening — otherwise we might thrash about during dreams. This disconnection of the motor impulses is the reason sleepwalking occurs only during non–REM sleep" (223).

Sleep paralysis, seen at the onset of sleep or in the first few moments after awakening from REM sleep, is not absolute. "If someone is very motivated to move or has strong feelings in the dream, the paralysis is occasionally overcome…. Nightmares commonly produce emotions strong enough to break through REM paralysis, although usually the movement or the emotion wakes the sleeper" (Dement and Vaughan, 1999, 294). Strong emotions are not restricted to nightmares, however.

"It may be that when there is a message from the dream world that really needs to get through, we are awakened when an intense emotion overcomes the sleep tendency and we wake up to realize we were dreaming"

(Dement and Vaughan, 1999, 307). Jung's theory on waking resembles that of the filmmaker. He writes in *Dreams* (1974): "We should not overlook the fact that the very dreams which disturb sleep most — and these are not uncommon — have a dramatic structure which aims logically at creating a highly affective situation, and builds it up so efficiently that the affect unquestionably wakes the dreamer" (38).

Artful Illusions

Bridging that murky gap between sleeping and waking is not as easy (or as glamorous) as it appears on film. A slowly shifting state of consciousness combined with a body still sluggish from sleep lethargy can make for a rude awakening in real life. Realistic awakenings on film likely would seem even ruder. In the movies, the transition is usually made by limber young women who miraculously spring out of bed maintaining their hairstyle and eye makeup from the night before, and by fast-acting men in boxer shorts who instantaneously recover from nocturnal penile tumescence. This artful illusion is embraced by audiences everywhere.

Film characters also have the amazing ability to overcome REM paralysis— especially upper body and vocal chords— by waking from disturbing dreams at the height of dramatic action. This trite waking-from-a-nightmare scene inevitably begins with the troubled sleeper lying flat on his or her back and then sitting up suddenly in bed with a shrill scream of terror. In the romantic comedy *Keeping the Faith* (1999), Father Brian Finn (Edward Norton) has an erotic dream about Anna Riley (Jenna Elfman), who is having a secret love affair with Finn's best friend. Without any stylistic cues to indicate the scene is a dream sequence, Brian and Anna are jogging through the park when she collapses from exhaustion and a sore leg muscle. As Brian massages and stretches her leg, she leans towards him and wipes a bead of sweat from his face. We hear the sound of his heartbeat pumping faster as the scene progresses. After seductively licking his sweat off her finger, she is revealed in a montage of quick flashbacks; they kiss passionately before he rips her shirt open. The next scene shows Brian, with several beads of sweat on his face, sitting up in bed, crying out in anguish as he awakens from his dream.

Although Brian's dream causes him to doubt his calling and to confess his love for Anna, he is neither the first nor the last (real or fictitious) Father to suffer from erotic dreams. The early Christian Father St. Augustine of Hippo used his dreams to channel communications between himself, God and the angels, repeatedly asking for chaste thoughts and desires.

"These images come into my thoughts, and, though when I am awake they are strengthless, in sleep they not only cause pleasure but go so far as to obtain assent and something very like reality. These images, though real, have such an effect on my soul, in my flesh, that false visions in my sleep obtain from me what true visions cannot when I am awake" (St. Augustine, 1963, 237).

Dream researcher Robert L. Van De Castle suggests that early church fathers such as St. Augustine battled the demons of lust in their dreams because of imposed celibacy, a question still debated today in light of sexual abuse charges within the Catholic Church. "Judging from autobiographical accounts, the Catholic saints were constantly tempted and struggled to remain vigilant against carnal desires. It would not be surprising if celibate priests frequently experienced seminal emission or 'pollution' dreams. Since Aristotle made no provision for unconscious libidinal drives to be expressed in dreams, the source of these foul and polluting dreams had to be attributed to an external source: the Devil" (Van De Castle, 1994, 84). Although the unfortunate Father Brian Finn does not blame the devil for sending this "foul and polluting" dream, he does receive sexual satisfaction from his nocturnal fantasy and finds the images retain their strength even upon awakening.

In *Lara Croft: Tomb Raider* (2001), thrill-seeking heiress Lara Croft (Angelina Jolie) needs no nocturnal fantasies to add excitement to her life. Instead, her dreams serve a distinctly different purpose; they give her a reason to seek more thrills in her waking life. In a prophetic dream, her dead father explains his bizarre theory of planetary alignment and time displacement, then requests that she save the world through a series of trips to faraway places where she can shoot guns, swing on ropes, dodge supernatural monsters, and engage in hand-to-hand combat with professional killers. Throughout the dream, intercuts show Lara restlessly tossing around in bed during REM sleep as a clock's ticking grows louder. Upon waking with the obligatory gasp at the height of action, she is instantly alert and grabs a knife hidden under her pillow for such occasions.

This ability to overcome REM immobility is not restricted to recently released light romantic comedies and big-budget action flicks, of course. Among the countless films that overlook paralyzed vocal chords and upper body movement for the sake of a dramatic awakening (and depiction of

Opposite: The dreams of Lara Croft (Angelina Jolie) can only pale in comparison to her real life adventures, which involve tight shirts and loose talk, long ropes and short fuses, big guns and small chances of survival in *Lara Croft: Tomb Raider* (Paramount Pictures, 2001). Photograph by Alex Bailey.

the characters' fitful sleep during the REM state) are the thrillers *Vertigo* (1958), *Marnie* (1964), *A Nightmare on Elm Street* (1984), *In Dreams* (1998), *Shattered Image* (1998), *The Sixth Sense* (1999), *Sleepy Hollow* (1999), *End of Days* (1999), and *Hollow Man* (2000); the dramas *Wild Strawberries* (1957), *Persona* (1966), *The Story of Adele H.* (1975), and *Ordinary People* (1980); the sci-fi action films *Dreamscape* (1984), *Total Recall* (1990), *Twelve Monkeys* (1995), and *Dark City* (1997); and the comedies *National Lampoon's European Vacation* (1984), *Pee-wee's Big Adventure* (1985), *Fletch* (1985), *The Princess Bride* (1987), *Raising Arizona* (1987), *Kindergarten Cop* (1990), *The Mask* (1994), *Analyze This* (1998), *Dudley Do-Right* (1999), and *Snow Dogs* (2002).

Awakenings

In artistic representation of sleep and dreams, some people literally wake up, others figuratively wake up and some are awakened at both levels as in the case of Prince Akeem of Zamunda (Eddie Murphy) in the John Landis–directed comedy *Coming to America* (1988). The film begins as he wakes on the morning of his twenty-first birthday (sans dream sequence), the day he will meet his arranged bride for the first time. He wakes the same way he does every morning: a twelve-piece musical ensemble playing softly in the balcony of his room acts as his alarm clock. After rising from his king-sized bed, the prince enjoys the services of the royal tooth brusher, the royal backside wiper, and the royal topless bathers.

Later in the day, Prince Akeem undergoes a different kind of awakening and rejects the antiquated marriage rites of his beloved Zamunda. "I want a woman that's going to arouse my intellect as well as my loins," he proclaims. The rest of the film follows his quest for a bride in Queens, New York.

An awakening — either with or without a dream sequence preceding it — is a device used by filmmakers of all genres to set the stage for coming attractions. In *Coming to America*, we do not need to see the dreams of Prince Akeem to recognize his symbolic awakening to new ideas about the traditions of his country. In *Groundhog Day* (1993), waking to the realization that he is stuck in a time loop until he gets things right is more significant to Bill Murray's character than his dream messages. Woody Allen's 1973 comedy *Sleeper*, in which a sleepy geek awakens after two hundred years, also uses waking up as a framework for focusing on the character's adjustments to his new world. The story of catatonic patients who respond to the drug L-dopa, *Awakenings* (1990) also places more emphasis on waking than sleeping.

However, in *Ordinary People*, a nightmare in the initial scene sets the tone and hints at the theme for the ensuing crisis and recovery of a troubled young man played by Timothy Hutton. In *Pee-wee's Big Adventure*, the film begins with a dream sequence of Pee-wee (Paul Reubens) racing his bicycle in Le Tour de France with a number zero pinned to the back of his jacket. He races past other contestants and wins a trophy, thus preparing the audience for the upcoming trauma of his stolen bicycle. Fellini's 1963 hallucinatory tale *8½* starts with a creepy dream sequence where a man is quietly smothering from fumes while trapped in his car on a gridlocked highway, indicating the movie's theme of a stifled director with no "direction" and nothing to say. *Dreamscape* begins with a horrific nightmare suffered by the president of the United States, a sequence that sets the entire plot into motion. Likewise, in *Total Recall*, a recurring nightmare about Mars at the beginning of the film instigates an amazing series of events.

The short experimental film *City Edition* (1980) ends with an awakening, which indicates that everything preceding the awakening was dreamed. These images include brief scenes from old black-and-white newsreels. Director Alan Berliner says his film ends with an awakening to help the viewer make sense of the implausible sequence of images. "Even though it's after the fact — that is, you don't know it's a dream until the end of the sequence when the man finally wakes up — it has the effect of calming the viewer down." He says awakening from the dream has a grounding effect because "it reflects back on and refers to its ineffable source of origin — the human mind, and the cinema's way of expressing one of its more fascinating dimensions."[9]

In films, suddenly

Filmmaker Alan Berliner says his short film *City Edition* ends with an awakening to help the viewer make sense of the implausible sequence of images presented in the old news footage. Photograph by Cori Wells Braun, courtesy of Alan Berliner.

awakening from a dream state can be dramatic and symbolic, but not usually scientific. Ignoring new discoveries of neuroscience and age-old knowledge of sleep paralysis, filmmakers concentrate exclusively on the poetry and drama of waking up, that momentary blurring of fact and fiction between the dreaming and waking states.

Dream Recall

Ironically, those blurry moments upon awakening are the best time to remember our dreams. Freud says that what we remember from a dream and then try to interpret becomes "mutilated by the unfaithfulness of our memory" and may be incomplete, untruthful, and false. "As on the one hand, we may doubt whether what we dreamed was really as disconnected as it is in our recollections, so on the other hand we may doubt whether a dream was really as coherent as our account of it; whether in our attempted reproduction we have not filled in the gaps which really existed, or those which are due to forgetfulness, with new and arbitrarily chosen material; whether we have not embellished the dream, rounded it off and corrected it, so that any conclusion as to its real content becomes impossible" (Freud, 1994, 370). Rather than discount a dream because of imperfect recall, he ignores these warnings because he has found "that the smallest, most insignificant, and most uncertain components of the dream-content invited interpretations no less emphatically than those which were distinctly and certainly contained in the dream" (370).

Jung provides a contrasting view of dream recall in which he relates dream recall to dream importance. "'Little' dreams are the nightly fragments of fantasy coming from the subjective and personal sphere, and their meaning is limited to the affairs of everyday. That is why such dreams are easily forgotten, just because their validity is restricted to the day-to-day fluctuations of the psychic balance. Significant dreams, on the other hand, are often remembered for a lifetime, and not infrequently prove to be the richest jewel in the treasure-house of psychic experience" (Jung, 1974, 76). Although dreams on film are usually of the "treasure-house" variety, and therefore remembered, actual dreams are not.

In *Twelve Monkeys* (1995), convict James Cole (Bruce Willis) is selected by his captors to travel back in time to research a deadly plague because of his highly developed observational skills. Although he can remember names and places as he jumps back and forth through time and has the wherewithal to collect evidence despite the desperate circumstances into which he is thrown, James has trouble recalling the specifics of his recurring dreams. Likewise, the audience has difficulty discerning whether the dreams are actually memories of the past or prophecies of the future.

This lack of total recall is what propels recurring dream sequences in films. As in the three-dream series in *Sleepy Hollow* (1999), each dream reveals more of the story and aids the character's understanding; otherwise there would be no point in remembering.

Humans spend one-third of their lives sleeping, with much of their sleep time spent dreaming, producing at least six dreams each night for a total of more than 150,000 dream dramas during a seventy-year life span, according to conservative estimates (Snyder, 1970). However, dream recall presents a significant problem because the varying stages of sleep are observable and their restorative benefits provable, but dream researchers must rely on the dreamer's memory for dream content, thereby limiting precise determination of a psychological function.

Poor dream recall is attributable to many causes, such as the subject's verbal proficiency, descriptive style, motivation, intelligence, and preconceptions that may impede accurate recollection of dream data. In *Dreaming Your Real Self* (1998), Joan Mazza suggests that dreams are difficult to relate because they appear in a jumbled, nonlinear form — incongruous to our natural way of thinking — making it difficult to retell the dream coherently or chronologically. The dreamer must "convert the simultaneous, confusing events and pictures into a linear, chronological order to catch the dream" and is more likely to remember "the dreams that terrify, repulse, puzzle, or leave us sexually aroused. Most dreams are not emotionally charged at all, so they fade from consciousness quickly" (Mazza, 22).

Physiological factors also may contribute to hazy dream recall; recent brain-imagery studies show the executive centers in the frontal cortex — important for self-awareness and voluntary action formation — are mostly inactive during REM sleep (Flanagan, 2000), and some researchers believe that dreaming is constructed more from visual memory stored in the right hemisphere than from a general long-term verbal left hemisphere memory (Antrobus, 1981). "In so-called nondreamers — who, it has been demonstrated, actually do dream — this memory shutdown is simply more complete than it is for the rest of the population. Even people who remember their dreams every night only remember the last several dreams they had before awakening" (Lewis, 1995, 156). Studies of people trying to learn new things such as a language while sleeping also indicate that the memory-recording processes of the brain do not function during sleep.

Science cannot provide a means of tapping into or accurately reproducing the conscious perception of the dreamer during a dream, so dreams are always out of time. "We have no direct access to dreaming consciousness, for the wrenching transition from dream to waking and the translation of memories into verbal description are subject to innumerable distorting influences" (Snyder, 1970, 126). Therefore dream descriptions are always in the past tense. "When a patient talks about his dream he is reporting something like a reconstituted text, something that happened in another state of mind and in another time frame. It no longer contains all the vital elements that are experienced and that constitute dream life. As a result, in the analytic process one is seeking to interpret the hidden meaning, but the interpretation is not the dream" (The Dalai Lama, 1997, 77).

In the futuristic sci-fi action film *Total Recall* (1990), Doug Quaid (Arnold Schwarzenegger) obsesses over the hidden meaning in his recurring dreams about Mars. In order to simulate a trip to Mars, he goes to a company called Recall that promises to implant the memories of someone else for the ultimate vacation experience. "Your brain will not know the difference," promises the salesman. However, during the implant process, Quaid suffers a "freeform paranoid delusion caused by a schizoid embolism"—at least that is what the Recall experts tell him. In truth, rather than reacting to memories from the new implant, he endures a rush of his own memories (such as those recalled in his dreams) that had been partially erased by a previous implant of which he is unaware.

In this special effects extravaganza, Quaid's remembered dreams are his forgotten reality and his new reality is an implanted dream. The bad guys (Ronnie Cox, Michael Ironside, and Sharon Stone) keep him (and the audience) as confused as possible in order to prevent total recall of his former identity. Remembering too much too early would eliminate the need for a hideous tracking device being extracted from his nose, a town full of mutant psychics, an elaborate alien-built reactor, a bloody arm-severing scene, the senseless murder of innocent goldfish, and a shocking plot twist near the end of the film.

Dream Time

As if actual dream recall were not complicated enough, dream recall in films has additional interpretive dimensions. The audience can view the dream in real-time as the dreamer is experiencing it (*In Dreams* [1999], *The Princess Bride* [1987], *Lara Croft: Tomb Raider* [2001]), thus obviating the character's need to remember. The dream can be reconstructed by the character and viewed by the audience (*Spellbound* [1945], *Wild Strawberries*

Director Paul Verhoeven (left) prepares Arnold Schwarzenegger for a scene in which his character has memories of Mars implanted into his brain so he can figure out the meaning of his dreams in *Total Recall* (Tri-Star Pictures, 1990).

[1957], *Marnie* [1964]). The character can give a verbal description of the dream based on memory or notes (*Final Analysis* [1992], *Analyze This* [1998], *End of Days* [1999]). Low-budget fare, such as the horror film *Phantasm II* (1988) save the time, money, and effort of actually producing a dream sequence (or even writing a description of a dream) by using creepy voiceovers from the deadly silver-sphere-wielding Tall Man (Angus Scrimm) while psychic teens are shown dozing and apparently experiencing expensive dream sequences in their heads.

Some characters such as Pee-wee Herman (Paul Reubens) appear to have no dream recall whatsoever. Pee-wee has three bizarre dream sequences in *Pee-wee's Big Adventure* (1985) that are memorable to the audience for their creative imagery, but are inconsequential and apparently forgotten by the character. Likewise, in the psychological thriller *Vertigo* (1958), Scottie (James Stewart) never mentions the very lengthy and terrifyingly vivid dream he experiences about falling from heights and falling in love. Stanley (Jim Carrey) in *The Mask* (1994) has a dream in which he fulfills his wishes for love, money, power, and success, yet wakes the next morning unchanged, on the same dangerous course of action as the night before the dream.

Terrifying nightmares that might scare other people can be summarily dismissed by scientists such as Dr. Linda McKay (Elisabeth Shue) in *Hollow Man* (2000) and Dr. Alan Grant (Sam Neill) in *Jurassic Park III* (2001). Although Linda dreams she is raped by an invisible man and Alan dreams he is trapped on an airplane with a talking velociraptor, the two doctors refuse to give in to superstition when they supposedly have science on their side. Both would have been safer listening to their unconscious warnings. Forgotten and disregarded dreams, such as these, explore the characters' psyche and aid plot development, thereby benefitting the audience rather than the film character.

Some people should not remember their dreams, and some dreams should not be remembered. Dreams can be "scary and embarrassing, and we'd rather forget them. Their memory raises uncomfortable or painful feelings we would prefer to avoid" (Mazza, 1998, 16). The overwhelming magnitude of dreams also proves a deterrent in effective dream recall. "If we remembered every dream clearly, it might become difficult to sort out what really occurred and what was a dream" (Dement and Vaughan, 1999, 298). With more than 150,000 potential dreams in a lifetime — most of which being nightly fragments of fantasy rather than rich jewels in the treasure-house — audience members do not need total recall of their own dreams, much less those of film characters who recite every mundane detail upon awakening. In the world of film, all dreams are rich jewels and a dream worth having is worth remembering — if not by the character, at least by the audience.

Part II

Creative Differences: Changes in Content

PATIENT: I'm still having these dreams, doctor, and I still can't stop myself from believing them.

PSYCHIATRIST: I've told you, Mr. Hofstetter, to believe in one's dreams is a manifestation of insanity and the sooner you accept this, the sooner you'll get well.

PATIENT: But I dreamed the archangel appeared and whispered into my ear and told me where to find a golden Wonka ticket.

PSYCHIATRIST: And what exactly did he say?

PATIENT: Well what difference does that make? This was a dream, a fantasy. I mean, you said yourself...

PSYCHIATRIST (shouting): Shut up, Hofstetter, and tell me where the ticket is!

— Scene from *Willy Wonka & the Chocolate Factory* (1971)

Chapter 7

Psychology of Sleeping and Dreaming

In *Spellbound* (1945), based on Francis Beeding's novel *The House of Dr. Edwardes*, psychiatrist Dr. Brulov (Michael Chekhov) believes he has dreams all figured out, based on his study of Freud. He tells JB (Gregory Peck) that correct dream analysis may cure his amnesia.

> I explain to you about dreams so you don't think it is hooey. The secrets of who you are and what has made you run away from yourself—all these secrets are buried in your brain…. They tell you what you are trying to hide. But they tell it to you all mixed up like pieces of a puzzle that don't fit. The problem of the analyst is to examine this puzzle and put the pieces together in the right place — and find out what the devil you are trying to say to yourself.

Alfred Hitchcock, director of the acclaimed film for which he and Chekhov were both nominated for Academy Awards, has vouched for the authenticity of the film's psychological elements. Although he says, "*Spellbound* was based on complete psychiatric truth" (Gottlieb, 1995, 114), the truth upon which the science is based appears to be strictly Freudian.

As shown in Part 1, understanding the physiology of sleep and phenomenological effects of the dreaming mind does not reveal the function and meaning of dreams. That is, we know *how* but are not sure *why* people dream. "The greatest insights into the functions of dreams are likely to arise from combining biological and psychological studies to determine the health benefits (or drawbacks) of having a conscious awareness of our inner selves as revealed through the dreaming mind" (Mazza, 1998, 167). Just as Freud theorized that form relates to content in dreams, perhaps the how and why of dreaming also are interdependent.

Activation-Synthesis

In *Dreaming Souls* (2000), Owen Flanagan outlines three current views on the function (the why) of dreams. The first view, the activation-synthesis model, explains dreams as unimportant noise created by awake experiences and thoughts combined with stimuli surrounding the dreamer, all interacting with memories and knowledge stored in areas activated by the random firings originating in the brain stem during sleep.

One popular theory of activation-synthesis explains REM sleep as disk maintenance, compression, trash disposal, and long-term memory consolidation, comparing the human mind to a computer. Pulitzer Prize-winning biologist Edward O. Wilson describes dreams as "the reorganization and editing of information in the memory banks of the brain" (1998, 75) and dream researcher Chester A. Pearlman, Jr., of Harvard Medical School suggests "that stage REM is involved in the formation of memory traces, reprogramming of the brain, integration of new experiences with existing personality, and so on" (1970, 331). According to this model, the unimportant noise caused by nightly interaction, compression, and reorganization produces meaningless dreams. However, in *Modern Man in Search of a Soul*, Jung warns of the dangers inherent with this kind of thinking: "Dreams can be anticipatory and, in that case, must lose their particular meaning if they are treated in a purely causalistic way" (1933, 7).

In *Willy Wonka & the Chocolate Factory*, a children's musical fantasy about figurative dreams of wealth, power, and enough free candy to rot a mouthful of teeth, the brief scene noted above portrays a psychiatrist who publicly endorses his own version of the activation-synthesis model (as discussed in Chapter 3), yet privately still believes that dreams are inherently meaningful. Interestingly, this film is based on the fanciful — and decidedly unscientific — book by Roald Dahl, and made six years before the theory of activation-synthesis was popularized by McCarley and Hobson in 1977.

Depth Psychology

A more popular view of dream function — especially among filmmakers— is based on Freud's original psychoanalytic dream theory also known as depth psychology, which characterizes dreams as deep thoughts serving two functions: The dream messages are disguised wishes that protect the mind and guard the sleep; and the release of these unconscious wishes frees the conscious mind to operate efficiently during the daytime. Only limited empirical research supports this theory, yet its proponents are many.

In *The Functions of Sleep and Memory Processing*, psychologist Ernest Hartmann writes, "In humans, although not all studies have found demonstrable psychological deficits, a number of small studies of D-deprivation [REM sleep] suggest irritability, poor social presence, defects in normal ego defensive functioning, and at times emergence of repressed impulses, wishes, and conflicts. This has been taken as supporting... Freud's view that the dream is a 'safety valve' of the mind" (1981, 113). Other experts also see value in Freud's original views. For example, Gerald Schoenewolf writes: "I agree with Freud that there is invariably a wish underneath almost every dream, whether that wish is direct (dreaming of food to satisfy hunger), indirect (dreaming of punishment to atone for guilt), or implied (dreaming of traumatic horror in order to master it)" (1997, 12). Robert Moss treats the dream message as an important cooperative function of the conscious and unconscious mind. "Dreaming, I am like the man in Plato's cave, who turns from watching the shadow play upon the wall and awakens to the source reality beyond appearance" (1998, 12).

Seeking the source reality beyond appearance (i.e., hidden meaning) represents the primary function of dreams on film. Filmmakers generally prefer the Freudian safety-valve approach to dream function whether these wishes are direct (in *Sleepless in Seattle* [1993], grief-stricken Sam Baldwin [Tom Hanks] dreams of his beloved dead wife talking to him), indirect (in *Analyze This* [1998], guilt-ridden mobster Paul Vitti [Robert DeNiro] dreams he gives black milk to a baby), or implied (in *Ordinary People* [1980] grief-stricken and guilt-ridden Conrad Jarrett [Timothy Hutton] dreams of a fatal boating accident in which his brother was killed). Because Conrad initially ignores the dream messages, his disguised wishes (that he should have died instead of his brother) intrude upon his waking life, thus impairing his efficiency during the daytime.

Theory of Mind

The third common view of dream function is the theory of mind, which comes in two forms. The first version describes the dreamer as a mind-reader, sorting through crucial information for better social interaction; the second version includes physiological aspects, describing dreaming as a mind-reading function (of ourselves and others) that coordinates with electrical activity originating in the brain stem associated with REM sleep that creates visual imagery. Flanagan compares the the-

Teenaged Conrad Jarrett (Timothy Hutton, right) reluctantly talks about his recurring nightmares with his psychiatrist (Judd Hirsch) in *Ordinary People* (Paramount Pictures, 1980).

ory of mind view with old television sets that used valve tubes rather than transistors. "These TVS would hum for awhile after the TV was turned off as the tubes crackled and cooled down... In one sense, sleep involves turning the system off, but some sort of humming — the hum of various kinds of dream mentation — persists through the night" (2000, 50).

Current research focuses more on this third view, which links the brain (activation-synthesis model) and mind (depth psychology) for determining dream function. Murray Gell-Man writes, "Where work does proceed on both biology and psychology and on building staircases from both ends, the emphasis at the biological end is on the brain (as well as the rest of the nervous system, the endocrine system, etc.), while at the psychological end the emphasis is on the mind — that is, the phenomenological manifestations of what the brain and related organs are doing" (1994, 117). Some scientists also theorize that while REM sleep reorganizes firing patterns in the central nervous system in response to the disorganizing effects of sleep, dreaming reorganizes patterns of ego defense and ego synthesis (Jones, 1970).

Combining Theories

Science fiction thrillers such as *Dreamscape* (1984) and *The Cell* (2000) tap into this more recent theory of physiology and psychology, using computers to monitor biological functions of dream-linkers while they explore the psychological depths of other people's dreams. Judging by the proliferation of cinematic tributes to Freudian and Jungian dream theories and the avoidance of breakthroughs in modern sleep science, *artistic* depiction of sleeping and dreaming *psychology* seems to interest filmmakers far more than *scientific* depiction of sleeping and dreaming *physiology.*

Henry Bromell, director of the psychological drama *Panic*, suggests one reason why modern filmmakers choose the former over the latter. "Older movies portrayed the emotional illness of characters more cautiously. There was something suspicious in our culture about psychology. A cartoony, simple-minded explanation was given to explain a character's behavior." But times have changed, he says. "In the present day, we have greater understanding of psychology — half of the filmmakers have been in therapy themselves."[10]

Despite all the theories, research, and technological advances, the function of the dreaming mind still eludes the scientific mind. Edward O. Wilson describes our knowledge of dreams as a mix of science and mysticism:

> Proximate explanations answer the question of how biological phenomena work, usually at the cellular and molecular levels. The second mode of explanation addresses why they work — their ultimate causes, which are the advantages the organism enjoys as a result of evolution that created the mechanisms in the first place.... To put the study of dreaming in a nutshell, we understand a good deal about the proximate causes of dreaming in general, but very little about its ultimate causes [1998, 79].

Sleep expert William C. Dement agrees. "Never before in the history of biology has so much been known about a phenomenon from the descriptive point of view while at the same time knowing so little about its function" (1970, 71).

Although resistant to scientific testing of laws and principles, and unable to be catalogued, organized, or examined under a microscope, dreams transcend time, space, and species for a reason. "Whatever its purpose, the intense activity of the dreaming brain is so important to us that the brain actively paralyzes the body's muscles to accommodate it" (Dement and Vaughan, 1999, 251).

Though important, the dreaming mind is playful as well. Jung says in *Dreams* (1974) that determining the borderline where play begins is no easy task because "the unconscious product is the creation of sportive fantasy, of that psychic impulse out of which play itself arises. It is repugnant to the scientific mind to indulge in this kind of playfulness, which tails off everywhere in inanity" (17). He cautions, however, to remember that the human mind has amused itself for thousands of years with this same kind of game, "so it would be no wonder if those tendencies from the distant past gained a hearing in dreams" (17).

More recently, as described in *Sleeping, Dreaming, and Dying* (1997), although REM sleep is a fundamental cognitive activity, it also provides:

> The place where people can engage in imaginary play, trying out different scenarios, learning new possibilities; a space of innovation where new patterns and associations can arise, where whatever was experienced can be re-elaborated... Dreaming provides a space where you don't just cope with immediacy, but instead can reimagine, reconceive, reconceptualize [35].

The intense activity of the dreaming brain also is so important (and so appealingly playful) that filmmakers routinely include dream sequences with images, insights, and information that must be interpreted—by a psychiatrist/psychologist, the dreamer, or the audience — to determine not *how*, but *why* the dreamer has these dreams.

Chapter 8

Dream Interpretation

In the horror classic *A Nightmare on Elm Street* (1984), a teenager plagued by nightmares of a hideously disfigured man with razor-sharp claws and a dirty red-and-green striped sweater is taken to the Katja Institute for the Study of Sleep Disorders. While young Nancy (Heather Langenkamp) lies on the hospital bed with electrodes strapped to her body, her nervous alcoholic mother (Ronee Blakely) asks the sleep scientist, "What the hell are dreams, anyway?" Providing an answer that would have made any other mother grab her daughter and run for a second opinion, Dr. King (Charles Fleischer) replies: "Mysteries. Incredible body hocus pocus. The truth is, we still don't know what they are or where they come from."

A genuine sleep scientist or mental health professional is not likely to calm patients' fears or solve their problems by describing recurrent nightmares as mysterious hocus pocus. In fact, a patient's spontaneous recitation of a dream might be interpreted as a sign of trust in the doctor or a narcissistic need to please. Sharing dreams represents part of the process of therapy; the actual dream content takes a secondary role (if that) in most clinical settings. Dreams are rarely solicited during psychotherapy except by strict followers of Freud, and then only after the patient-therapist relationship is well-established enough to obtain a knowledgeable interpretation of what those particular dreamed images may mean on that particular day to that particular dreamer within the context of his other shared dreams.

Experts currently downplay the significance of dreams and emphasize the artistic, as opposed to the scientific, aspects of dream interpretation. Owen Flanagan writes, "Although there are credible adaptationist accounts for sleep and phases of the sleep cycle itself, there is reason to think that the phenomenal mentation, the dreaming, that occurs during sleep is a good example of a by-product of what the system was designed to do while awake and during sleep and sleep cycling" (2000, 87). He further describes dreams as epiphenomena "in the sense that they are serendipitous accompaniments of what sleep is for" (2000, 115).

Dement compares dreaming to the images seen through a stained glass window. "As random signals travel through the brain, they are modified and filtered by the brain's current state... White light, which is a jumble of all colors, enters on one side, but what comes out on the other side has a definite pattern of colors that is often very meaningful. Like the stained glass window (which is a filter for light), the brain acts as a filter that imposes order on the random signals passing through it" (Dement and Vaughan, 1999, 304). He concludes that whether unconscious or not, our experiences of the day combined with our life experiences, "form the 'stained glass' that filters incoming signals—and creates the vivid landscapes of dreams" (305).

If we create our own "vivid landscapes" in dreams, then it would take an artist to fully appreciate them, according to Gerald Schoenewolf in *The Dictionary of Dream Interpretation* (1997). "The interpretation of dreams remains an art, just as does the interpretation of a poem, a parable, or a painting ... even the interpretations of the most learned art critics disagree with one another, and so too do the interpretations of the most well-trained psychoanalysts and psychotherapists" (12).

Repressed Desires

Incorporating "scientific" dream interpretation into the clinical setting, however, was standard practice for Freud and his early followers. He writes, "There is a psychological technique which makes it possible to interpret dreams, and that on the application of this technique, every dream will reveal itself as a psychological structure, full of significance, and one which may be assigned to a specific place in the psychic activities of the waking state" (Freud, 1994, 3). This technique involves deciphering disguised dream messages through free association to release the conscious mind from the repressed desires of the unconscious mind, thus healing emotional illness. Psychoanalysis is a method for interpreting the remembered dream by reconstructing its cause, i.e., using the manifest content as a path to the latent content — the true meaning buried within the story dream.

The Alfred Hitchcock films *Spellbound* (1945) and *Marnie* (1964) rely on Freudian dream interpretation to conveniently solve complex sets of problems in the final minutes of the movies. The manifest contents of the

dreams—earlier revealed to the dreamer, and, of course, the audience—
become secondary to the more important latent contents revealed by
insightful interpretation. In *Spellbound*, dream interpretation using free
association reveals where, why, and how a murder occurs. Similarly in
Marnie, dream interpretation also helps a young woman heal her childhood wounds surrounding a murder. Both films depict Freud's theory of
disguised symbols representing implied wishes where the dreamer relives
the traumatic horror in order to master it.

A Dream from the Archives

More recently, in the Phil Joanou–directed thriller *Final Analysis*
(1992), Freudian dream interpretation literally resolves the movie's conflict.
The film begins with emotionally troubled patient Diana Evans (Uma
Thurman) recounting this dream to her psychiatrist, Dr. Isaac Barr
(Richard Gere): "I had the dream again. I'm arranging flowers on a table
for a centerpiece. I decorate the flower pot with fancy paper. It feels like
velvet. There are three different kinds of flowers. There are lilies, and there
are ... by the way, did you reach my sister?" In a later scene, she relates
the dream again, this time revealing lilies and carnations in the arrangement. Still later, Diana says "I had the dream again," and includes violets,
although she first mispronounces the word as "violence," then "violates."

Dr. Barr, however, is far more interested in illicit affairs than in elic-
iting information. Obsessed with Diana's sister, Heather (Kim Basinger),
he fails to notice the Freudian dream symbols until he attends a lecture
about Freud's views on women and hears the speaker describe one patient's
dream about arranging flowers on a table. The speaker even mentions that
the reference is found in Chapter Six of *The Interpretation of Dreams*, thus
enabling Dr. Barr quick and easy access to the passage when he races to
the library located next door to the lecture hall.

Sure enough, in section E of Chapter Six, he finds the same dream
listed under "Representation in Dreams by Symbols: Some Further Typical Dreams" (Freud, 1994, 238). He learns (too late) that Diana's dream
is actually the recorded dream of "a non-neurotic girl of a rather prudish
and reserved type" (255) who dreams of lilies to represent purity, carnations to symbolize carnal desire, and violets to stand in for women's supposed need to be violated violently. After Dr. Barr consults Freud's dream
interpretation, he realizes he was duped by Diana and Heather to cover
up a killing.

After the murderous Heather takes a final flying leap off a lighthouse

tower, Dr. Barr tells Diana that because of the dream, he knew all along that she really wanted to help him, not help Heather.

"You wanted me to recognize it," he says. "Consciously or not, you wanted me to know everything." Yet he remains troubled. "Why did you pick a dream from the archives?"

She answers him sharply (still maintaining the Freudian perspective that dreams are "full of significance"): "Because *my* dreams are none of your business."

Books on dream interpretation are unlikely to provide help in understanding symbols from a dream from the archives or a dream as recent as last night. For example, *A Dictionary of Dreams* (1992), originally published in 1909, says if we dream of smoke it "foretells that you will be perplexed with doubts and fears. To be overcome with smoke, denotes that dangerous persons are victimizing you with flattery" (516). *Understanding and Interpreting Dreams* (1990) says to dream of "slow, twisting smoke is a warning of death" (228). *The Dream Encyclopedia* (1995) says "to be surrounded by smoke in a dream indicates that the dreamer is suffering from confusion and anxiety. Often a dreamer will be choked and disoriented suggesting the need to 'clear things up'" (353). Actually dreaming of a smoking gun or cigar-smoking psychiatrist may represent nothing more than the obvious representation, because as Freud says, sometimes a cigar is just a cigar — a symbol which curiously is not contained in any of the three books mentioned above. Dreams on film ignore the individual relevance of dream symbols, and instead rely on a collective unconscious and a shared artistic consciousness that define all dream symbols similarly, so that a smoking gun is likely a phallic symbol or sexual gratification, and a cigar-smoking psychiatrist a symbol of repressed sexuality.

The Collective Unconscious

Dream interpretations on film are not loyal to Freudian theories alone. The Jungian concept of the collective unconscious also finds its way into the collective conscious that is depicted on film. In *Modern Man in Search of a Soul* (1933), Jung writes, "The evolutionary stages through which the

Opposite: In *Final Analysis*, psychiatrist Dr. Isaac Barr (Richard Gere) is so busy courting his patient's sister (Kim Basinger) that he fails to notice that the disturbed young woman's dreams come directly from Freud's *The Interpretation of Dreams* (Warner Bros., 1992).

human psyche has passed are more clearly discernible in the dream than in consciousness. The dream speaks in images, and gives expression to instincts, that are derived from the most primitive levels of nature"(26). In *Dreams* (1974), he claims that dream images provide unconscious complements to our conscious situation of the moment through a shared pool of archetypal images (35), and further concludes that a dream is a product of the total psyche comprised of "everything that has ever been of significance in the life of humanity" (63).

Such is the case in the eight dream sequences comprising the entire film *Akira Kurosawa's Dreams* (1990). Based on Kurosawa's own dreams, the sequences depict mythical creatures including vengeful foxes that marry, trees that take on human form, dead soldiers marching from a tunnel, a beautiful winter wind spirit who appears during a blizzard, and a ragged one-horned demon mutated from nuclear fallout.

The book *VideoHound's Golden Movie Retriever* (2001) describes Kurosawa's stories as anthological lessons "regarding the simultaneous loss of humanity and nature" that "although startling and memorable" come

The Snow Fairy (Mieko Harada, top) brings warmth and comfort to a lost mountain man (Akira Terao) during "The Blizzard," one of several dream sequences using mythological creatures that comprise *Akira Kurosawa's Dreams* (Warner Bros., 1990).

In the dream sequence "Sunshine Through the Rain," a parade of foxes perform a musical wedding march through the forest as a young boy risks his life to watch the forbidden event in *Akira Kurosawa's Dreams* (Warner Bros., 1990).

across as "strangely trite" and lack the power normally associated with his work (Craddock, 56). Jung writes in *The Spirit in Man, Art, and Literature* (1966): "The primordial image, or archetype, is a figure — be it a daemon, a human being, or a process— that constantly recurs in the course of history and appears wherever creative fantasy is freely expressed" (81). Out of a lifetime of dreams, Kurosawa likely selects familiar archetypes so he can empower his film with universal messages from our collective unconscious.

Dormant Memories

Although *Cat People* (1982), *Dark City* (1997), and *The Matrix* (1999) also explore themes of the collective unconscious, Jungian ideas are best represented in *Altered States*, Ken Russell's 1980 hallucinogenic tale of an obsessive professor who ingests toxic mushrooms and sleeps in an isolation tank in order to invoke ancient primordial memories through dream states. In his search for the "real self," Dr. Eddie Jessup (William Hurt) takes over a research laboratory at Harvard Medical School where sleep studies have been performed. Not content with test subjects, he experiments on himself in order to get in touch with "six million years of memories" that lay dormant inside him, echoing Jung's theory that "the journey through the psychic history of mankind has as its object the restoration of the whole man, by awakening the memories in the blood" (Jung, 1966, 140).

Dr. Jessup's belief that "altered states of consciousness can be as real as a waking state," his earlier childhood visions of Christ and the saints, the mushrooms, and the tank make a dangerous mix. His hallucinations of primitive man become externalized, and he eventually undergoes a complete physical and psychological regression that turns him into a hairy ape-like creature who terrorizes a security guard and wreaks havoc at the zoo. *Altered States* begins with a literal scene of Dr. Jessup waking up in the tank and ends with his figurative awakening. Fed up with searching for the ultimate truth, devouring goats for dinner, and enduring that uncomfortable process of genetic regression, he realizes that what is real

Dr. Eddie Jessup (William Hurt) endures the uncomfortable process of genetic regression in order to tap into six million years of memories in *Altered States* (Warner Bros., 1980).

is transitory, i.e., the here, the now, and his love for his wife (Blair Brown). In discovering Jung's shared pool of the collective unconscious, Dr. Jessup interprets his own dreams and finds the pool is shallow, dry, and empty.

Whether interpreted by a psychiatrist (*Spellbound* [1945], *Willy Wonka & the Chocolate Factory* [1971], *Ordinary People* [1980], *Final Analysis* [1992], *Twelve Monkeys* [1995], *Analyze This* [1998], *Vanilla Sky* [2001]); a "nearly certified hypnotherapist" (*Stir of Echoes* [1999]), the dreamers themselves (*Wild Strawberries* [1957], *In Dreams* [1998], *Lara Croft: Tomb Raider* [2001]); or the audience (*Persona* [1966], *The Story of Adele H.* [1975], *Raising Arizona* [1987], *Living in Oblivion* [1994]), dreams on film are designed for interpretation.

Dreams on television (at least in Turkey) are not designed for interpretation, however. The Turkish Radio and Television High Council announced a ban on the interpretation of dreams on television recently, citing an anti-social effect in which "the public is misinformed and dragged into fatalism" (Andrews, 2000, 2). The council said airing dream interpretations is illegal and violates broadcasting regulations. If this ban is ever broadened to include the interpretation of dreams on film, hundreds of the finest movies ever made would never enter the collective conscious of the film-going public.

Chapter 9

Altered States of Consciousness

Unlike Dr. Jessup (William Hurt) in *Altered States* (1980), most of us can obtain altered states of consciousness without ingesting toxic mushrooms, floating naked in isolation tanks, or experiencing genetic regression. Likewise, Craig Schwartz (John Cusack) and his scheming associates in *Being John Malkovich* (1999) take things a little too far by charging customers $200 for a fifteen-minute trip through a magic portal that enters the consciousness of actor John Malkovich (who plays himself in the film). Even without the benefit of isolation tanks and magic portals, we can — and do — shift between altered states of consciousness all day, every day.

"Dreaming is surely different from our waking consciousness. Most people think of themselves as having only three states of consciousness: awake, asleep, and dreaming. But when we are awake, there are literally thousands of altered states of consciousness (ASCs) that most people experience regularly" (Mazza, 1998, 180). Watching a movie, reading a book, playing with an infant, concentrating on a puzzle, playing a musical instrument, having a temper tantrum, experiencing an anxiety attack, or engaging in a sexual fantasy all require shifts in consciousness. "Dreaming is one of many of these states, a natural altered state of consciousness. But even dreaming has various levels... Conscious dreaming, also called lucid dreaming, is different from the dreams we have when we don't know we are dreaming" (181).

Sleep expert Ernest Hartmann, of Tufts University School of Medicine in Boston, describes a continuum of mental functioning with focused waking thought on one end and dreaming on the other. Focused waking thought deals with perceptual input, math symbols, signs, and words according to his theory. Next comes looser, less-structured waking thoughts with fewer words and signs, but more visual-spatial imagery. This second phase can return to focused waking thought or drift further

For $200, visitors can enter a magic portal that takes them into the consciousness of John Malkovich in *Being John Malkovich* (USA Films, 1999).

towards dreaming with thoughts described by Hartmann as reverie, free association, or daydreaming. The fourth and final phase in the continuum is dreaming, which deals with almost pure imagery and pictorial metaphor.

In addition to the form of thoughts expressed, a significant difference in self-reflection is evident throughout the phases. As mentioned in the Preface, the similarity between films and dreams makes the movies themselves good tools for measuring the waking-dreaming continuum. Focused waking thought is highly self-reflective with full and conscious knowledge of our presence within our surroundings: *I am sitting in the movie theater with my date, eating my popcorn, and waiting for the film* Being John Malkovich *to begin.* Looser, less structured waking thought and reverie, free association, and daydreaming produce a less self-reflective perception of our presence: *I am happy, uncomfortable, angry, and lustful as I feel other characters experiencing these feelings through the consciousness of John Malkovich.* In typical dreams, i.e., non-lucid REM dreams, the dreamer is completely there in the dream with no self-reflection: *I am John Malkovich.*

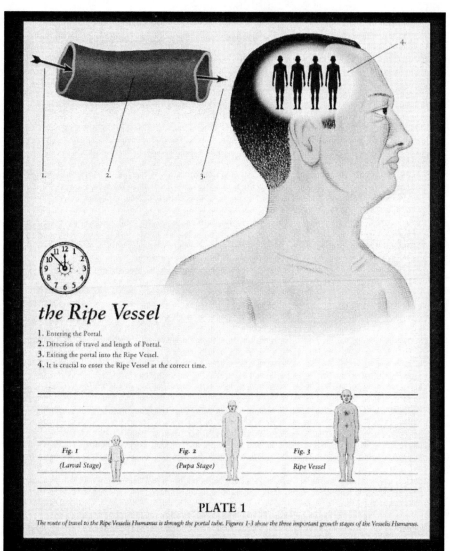

A Continuum of Consciousness

Hartmann says one of the main differences between altered states of consciousness is how much metaphor is involved in connecting ideas during processing.

> As we move along our continuum from focused waking thought — doing arithmetic problems — to daydreaming and dreaming, our mental processing becomes increasingly metaphoric. We may be able to do a problem in arithmetic or logic without using metaphor, but we are incapable of lying back and daydreaming about life or death without metaphor. Even less are we able to dream without using metaphor. We use metaphor in storing and processing all our important notions and concepts [Hartmann, 2000, 70].

Although animals likely use a language other than metaphor, Hartmann's theory supports recent findings by researchers studying rat brains during sleep, which offer evidence that patterns of brain activity identified during the day while awake are reproduced during the night while asleep. "In particular, the patterns, detected in the firing clusters of cells in the hippocampus, an area involved with memory formation and storage, were reproduced during phases of sleep that in humans are strongly linked to dreaming" (Goode, 2001, A-16). This study lends support to the idea that sleep plays a critical role in the encoding and storage of memories, and for the first time demonstrates "that complex episodic memories are being replayed or 'rehearsed' in the hippocampus during sleep, perhaps representing a process by which memory is gradually consolidated and passed to other parts of the brain" (A-16). In short, modern science links altered states of consciousness with different types of thought processing necessary for encoding and storage.

Dreaming — associated with REM sleep, brain-stem activation, and muscular inhibition — is not completely restricted to these conditions, however. "The biology of the mental state 'dreaming' must be a biological state at the cortex that is perhaps most commonly, or most readily, produced by the conditions of REM sleep but which can also be produced at other times — frequently at sleep onset and occasionally during wakefulness; perhaps at times of daydreaming or reverie, including 'artistic' reverie ... and also in psychedelic drug states, among others" (Hartmann, 2000, 66). In *Sleeping, Dreaming, and Dying* (1997), The Dalai Lama writes: "You

Opposite: A promotional postcard for *Being John Malkovich* portrays a ripe vessel for expanding our continuum of consciousness (in cinematic terms) (USA Films, 1999).

can be awake and hallucinate; you can have hypnagogic images when you're falling asleep; you can have dreams with mental content in non–REM sleep; and you can have classic dreams in REM sleep. But if we define dreaming strictly as vivid, storylike, with a continuous plot, then it's more of a REM phenomenon"(42–43). Although we have come a long way since Freud's claim that "day-dreams are the immediate predecessors of symptoms of hysteria," (Freud, 1994, 353) current sleep science contains more guidelines, observations, and theories about the dreaming states than actual rules.

This hazy, subjective continuum of consciousness translates well to film where the difference between flashbacks, fantasies (daydreams), hallucinations, and dreams are often indistinguishable and irrelevant to the viewer. In which altered state does Dr. Jessup in *Altered States* find himself when he gets in touch with "six million years of memories" after taking hallucinogenic mushrooms and immersing himself in an isolation tank where he closes his eyes and rests? How can we tell who is more unstable in Ingmar Bergman's psychological drama *Persona* (1966): the psychiatric patient with selective mutism or her nurse who guzzles liquor, reads other people's mail, and suffers a breakdown characterized by a blur of youthful memories, homoerotic fantasies, bizarre hallucinations, and disturbing dreams?

In addition to this overlap in form, the content of these altered states also blends together. Diffused light, soft focus, echoes, sound distortion, and color changes (such as shifts to black and white, monochrome, or saturated color) may represent the content style; a melding of past, present, and future or a confusion between reality and illusion may represent the content substance. Neither the style nor substance reliably predict whether the content represents a waking dream, a dreamy wakefulness, or something else altogether.

Because of the overlap in various altered states depicted on film, perhaps the best way to distinguish between artistically inspired flashbacks, fantasies, hallucinations, and dreams is by their relationship to the science of sleep. *Flashbacks* are real memories relived while awake. *Fantasies* are unfulfilled wishes experienced as waking dreams. *Hallucinations* are wishful or fearful waking fantasies experienced as reality by the person experiencing them. *Dreams* are flashbacks, fantasies, and hallucinations experienced while asleep.

Flashbacks

Although many films such as *Wild Strawberries* (1957), *Persona* (1966), *Despair* (1977), *Altered States* (1980), *Twelve Monkeys* (1995), and *The Cell*

(2000) combine a variety of altered states to fuse time, place, events, and people, other films clearly delineate the dream states of the characters. In the psychological drama *Panic* (2000), director-writer Henry Bromell uses several flashbacks to reveal more about the central character Alex (William H. Macy), a mild-mannered hitman enduring a mid-life crisis in which he questions the value of his chosen profession. Although Alex complains that "I'm asleep on my damn feet," his only dreams are daydreams about the past.

With no special visual effects to signify an altered state of consciousness, these flashbacks shift back and forth through time, relying on the psychological development of the characters and their age progression/regression as identifying elements. The flashbacks recall real memories from Alex's childhood, such as when his gangster father taught him how to kill a person by shooting a squirrel. When he discovers that his father also has trained his seven-year-old son to kill a squirrel, Alex mixes his own flashback with an imagined flashback of his son, alternating between past images of himself as a boy and current images of his son. The impact of this fantasy of a flashback within a flashback depends entirely on the content, rather than the form, of the recalled and relived memory.

The flashbacks in this film reveal the magnitude of the family's dysfunction. "The title refers to the internal panic felt by Macy's character," Bromell says. "This is a very dysfunctional family and he learns how hard it is to break out of the habits of that family" (Halpern, 2000, 58). Bromell, who previously directed episodes of television's *Chicago Hope, Homicide, Northern Exposure* and *I'll Fly Away*, says he instinctively knows whether to use a flashback or dream sequence to reveal the psychological state of a character. "The flashbacks progress from shooting his first squirrel to shooting his first person. I needed to reveal these crucial scenes from the past and used flashbacks to do it. Dreams are really tough to do well and can seem hokey if they aren't done right."[11]

Fantasies

In *American Beauty* (1999), unfulfilled wishes experienced as waking dreams contrast the concupiscent fantasy world of Lester Burnham (Kevin Spacey) with his withered reality. Trapped in a miserable job and an unhappy marriage, Lester (like Alex) endures a debilitating mid-life crisis in this Sam Mendes–directed film that won five Academy Awards in 1999, including Best Picture. His sexual fantasies and erotic daydreams about his daughter's high school classmate increase in frequency and intensity as his desperation grows. The lighting, zooms, close-ups, distorted sound, musical themes, and unlikely content (erotic wish fulfillment) of his fantasies are dreamlike; the only difference between these fantasy sequences and hundreds of filmed dream sequences is that Lester is awake — though in an altered state — while experiencing them.

Similarly, Clark W. Griswold (Chevy Chase) in *National Lampoon's Vacation* (1985) experiences erotic fantasies of himself with a beautiful woman (Christie Brinkley) in a red sports car. Like Lester, Clark fails to actualize his fantasy when given the opportunity.

Hallucinations

Hallucinations are wishful or fearful waking fantasies mistaken for reality by the person experiencing them. In the drama *Despair* (1977), adapted from Vladimir Nabokov's novel about a delusional owner of a failing chocolate factory, Hermann Hermann (Dirk Bogarde) experiences dreamlike hallucinations in which he makes love to his wife in bed, while simultaneously watching the spectacle from a nearby chair. Middle-aged with an average build, Hermann also believes that a young, tall, muscled day laborer who looks nothing like him is his exact physical double.

Much of the film is shot through windows or peeking from behind doors, indicating a separation from reality. Hermann's dreams, hallucinations, and delusions serve as visual proof of his mental deterioration as he plans a murder/merger (he keeps confusing the two in his explanations) to turn his failing business and lackluster personal life around. Like dreams on film, however, hallucinations on film reveal only partial details, sometimes disguised or out of sequence in order to aid plot development. Inch by inch, Hermann's hallucinations (and dreams) reveal the who, what, when, where, why, and how of his intended murder/merger plans.

Dreams

In terms of form and content, flashbacks, fantasies, and hallucinations on film resemble dreams on film except that in dreams the person is asleep while in an altered state of consciousness. These altered states often appear within the dreams themselves. In *Sleepy Hollow* (1999), Tim Burton's dark rendition of the classic Washington Irving tale of the headless horseman, Ichabod Crane (Johnny Depp) experiences flashbacks in his dreams in which he relives his beloved mother's persecution for witchcraft.

These flashbacks provide the basis for his current obsession with science and repression of the supernatural and establish his attraction for Katrina Van Tassel (Christina Ricci), a younger version of his mysterious mother. "If one can imagine someone with narcolepsy living in Medieval time, all of the symptomatology would seem supernatural. Even in today's world, the sleep-onset REM period dreams are often confused with reality" (Dement and Vaughan, 1999, 199). Perhaps Ichabod (who can fall asleep and dream at a moment's notice), his mother, and Katrina were actually persecuted because they suffered from an undiagnosed sleep disorder that caused them to behave and believe outside of the norm.

In another Burton film, *Pee-wee's Big Adventure* (1985), Pee-wee Herman (Paul Reubens) has a fantasy dream in which he fulfills his wish of racing his bicycle in the Tour de France and winning a trophy. The smooth ride in his dream can only be a dream, however, for Pee-wee cannot even pedal around town without taking a spill. Until the devastating theft of his vintage red bicycle, he races around town in a vain attempt to make his dream a reality.

Hallucinatory dreams contain the same wishful or fearful content of fantasies, but are experienced as reality by the person dreaming them. This concept is especially confusing because all dreamers believe their dreams are real while they are dreaming. However, a hallucinatory dream implies some degree of lucidity (see Chapter 16), i.e., the dreamer realizes that he or she is in a dream, yet believes that the consequences of the dream are real. In *Dreamscape* (1984), Alex Gardner (Dennis Quaid) and his psychic dream-linking nemesis go into other people's dreams— one as savior and one as assassin. Both men know they are in a dream —created by the dreamer, but developed by the intrusive dream-linkers— yet they believe that death within the dream means death in reality. Their hallucinations within the dream become a dangerous reality.

The hallucinatory dream of a dead child greeting the dying parent is especially poignant and popular in modern film. *Jacob's Ladder* (1990), *In Dreams* (1998), and *End of Days* (1999) all use this image during the final scenes where long-lost angelic offspring encourage dying parents to hold their hands and walk towards the light.

In *Stranger* (2000), director-writer-actor Scott Crowell uses a mixture of flashbacks, fantasies, hallucinations, and dreams to chronicle the past and present life of a nameless drifter through a nonlinear plot structure that flashes backward and forward through time in a storyline as meandering as the stranger himself. A stream of consciousness narrative with virtually no dialogue tells of the stranger's disturbing journey and the people he meets along the way (Halpern, 2001). Dream-like sequences

with garbled sound, diffused lighting, and sepia tones, slowly explain the abusive past that led to the stranger's present condition. Through childhood memories, fantasies, drug-and-psychosis-induced hallucinations, and a closed-eye dream state, the stranger shares his past, present, and future with us.

Crowell says he uses these altered states of consciousness as creative tools to heighten interest. These techniques develop characters, reflect change in characters, keep the plotline going, and show how history repeats itself. On the other hand, Crowell says these creative tools can distance audience members who dislike time dis-

A nameless drifter (Scott Crowell) tells his story in shifting streams of consciousness including flashbacks, fantasies, hallucinations, and dreams in *Stranger* (Firebrand Films, 2000). Courtesy of Scott Crowell.

placement and filmmaker tricks. "One of the golden rules of filmmaking is 'Don't use flashbacks,' but, of course, that's coming from some attorney in Hollywood who's only concerned about the bottom line."[12] Golden rule or not, filmmakers continue to use dream-like flashback, fantasy, and hallucinatory sequences, in addition to actual dreams, to portray altered states of consciousness in small independent films, multi-million-dollar studio blockbusters and everything in between.

In the world of film, humans are not the only creatures capable of altering their state of mind. In the anthropomorphic children's fantasy films *Babe* (1995) and *Gordy* (1995), talking pigs not only have vivid flashbacks, fantasies, and dreams, but the ability to outsmart some of the humans. In the family comedy *See Spot Run* (2001), Spot the dog (a.k.a. Agent 11) works as one of the country's top FBI agents. Though unable to speak, he can sniff out drugs, retrieve stolen purses, castrate mob bosses, and most importantly, have flashbacks to his days as a puppy.

In these flashbacks, he remembers the exact words of his trainer scolding him as a "bad dog" for wanting to play instead of work. He not only remembers, but relives the experience with the accompanying sense of guilt and shame. Because all mammals (except the anteater) experience REM and non–REM sleep and have been shown to dream, the concept of a canine flashback is not inconceivable. A dog's learned behavior is linked to memory which is linked to flashbacks which are linked to dreams. Dogs can learn, remember, and dream, but are unlikely to relive emotional experiences and remember language they can neither speak nor understand.

Unconcerned with studying firing clusters of cells in the brains of sleeping rats or exploring the logic of wordy canine flashbacks, filmmakers are far more concerned with the metaphoric language, stunning visuals, and other creative potential found in altered states of consciousness. As Freud writes in *Civilization and Its Discontents* (1961), the connection with reality is loosened by our internal, psychical processes. "Satisfaction is obtained from illusions, which are recognized as such without the discrepancy between them and reality being allowed to interfere with enjoyment" (31). Filmmakers, such as Ingmar Bergman, Sam Mendes, and Tim Burton, fully achieve their objective of audience satisfaction through depiction of altered states in which the discrepancy between a filmic flashback, fantasy, hallucination, or dream and the actual experience becomes momentarily irrelevant for the sake of their art.

Chapter 10

Visions and Prophesies

In *Twelve Monkeys* (1995), time-traveling convict James Cole (Bruce Willis) has five dreams in which he sees a mustached man in a flowered shirt and a blond woman wearing sunglasses walking through an airport. A terrified young boy watches as the man is shot dead. Because the boy in the dream is James in 1996 and the man in the dream is the time-traveling James of 2035, are these experiences—which he partially remembers in his waking state—visions, flashbacks within a dream, prophecies, or precognitions? Most cinematic dream states defy simple categorization; this is doubly true in a cerebral Terry Gilliam-directed fantasy such as *Twelve Monkeys*.

On film, visions and prophecies (referring specifically to the subject of the dreamlike state) are even harder to differentiate than flashbacks, fantasies, hallucinations, and dreams (which primarily refer to the state of consciousness in which the dream/vision is experienced). The fact that visions can be revealed through flashbacks, fantasies, and hallucinations, and that predictive dreams, which may be prophetic or precognitive, are believed to originate from an unknown supernatural source outside of the dreamer complicates the issue even further.

According to *The Dream Encyclopedia* (1995) the differences between these dream messages are subtle: *visions* predict the future and are experienced while awake; *prophetic dreams* predict the future of important events over which we have some control to change, and are experienced while asleep; *precognitive dreams* predict the future of trivial events over which we have no control, and are experienced while asleep. Prophetic and precognitive dreams may be considered divine, i.e., highly symbolic dreams originating from God or an angel. Divine dreams are rare in the movies because most of us consider ourselves honest and decent, so we feel more personally connected watching a good person (like ourselves) being tempted by evil, than an evil person being tempted by good.

Audience involvement and connectedness are, of course, the main reasons for including dreams and other altered states of consciousness in films.

In the Realm of the Metaphysicians

Modern science has little to say about visions and prophecies and leaves this realm open for exploration by metaphysicians. Opinions such as those expressed by Joan Mazza in *Dreaming Your Real Self* (1998) echo sentiments by sleep scientists, dream researchers, and scholars. "Dreams often appear to be a prophecy because we are aware at a deeper level of our being ... of where our present path will lead us. If we continue our behaviors in our relationships, at work, or in the way we care for our bodies, we know what the outcome will be... These dream warnings might come as you begin to be aware of a deterioration in your physical health, the security of your job, or the stability of your relationships" (13). Current scientific thought explains predictive dreams as originating from the psyche because of logical and reasonable observations during our waking hours. However, in previous times, dreams and visions that foreshadowed events fell under the jurisdiction of religion rather than science.

Attributing dream origin to a natural inner source inside the dreamer, i.e., the unconscious mind, instead of an unknown supernatural outside source is a relatively new idea. From ancient times until the late 1800s, dreams were viewed primarily as messages from an external source, either from God, demons, or physical causes. In these earlier times, whether literal or symbolic, messages believed to be from God were dreams/visions of a predictive nature; dream messages delivered by demons offered temptation; other dreams inspired by physical functioning were prompted by current external stimuli such as weather, temperature, and environment. Regardless of their source of origin, dreams are powerful, important and accessible, offering a free potential source of wisdom and guidance to every person regardless of age, race, sex, education, socioeconomic bracket or level of spiritual development.

Nowhere is the power, importance and accessibility of dreams more apparent than in the Bible, whose heroes and villains receive countless predictive messages, primarily in the form of visions and predictive dreams. Originally published in 1909, *A Dictionary of Dreams* (1992) claims, "The prophets and those who have stood nearest the fountain of universal knowledge used dreams with more frequency than any other mode of divination" (Miller, 7). Predictive dreams are common throughout the Bible, with dreams and waking visions considered to be gifts from God.

> The Talmud, the collected commentary on biblical text that, along with the Old Testament is part of the foundation of the Jewish religion, also mentions the use of dreams to predict the future, citing the potential of dreams to influence the decisions of kings and governments. Compiled between 200 B.C. and 300 A.D., the Talmud discusses the purpose of dreams extensively, purporting that dreams have meaning subject to interpretation and serving as a notable precursor to some contemporary theories [Koch-Sheras and Lemley, 1995, 27].

The Talmud expresses two different kinds of dream interpretation: that dreams come from higher powers and that dreams are generated by the psyche. "Interestingly, the Talmud also contains references to dreams as wish fulfillment, which is how Sigmund Freud would later characterize all dream content" (Koch-Sheras and Lemley, 27).

The predictive nature of dreams was accepted in the ancient world, although acceptance of the dreamer was not guaranteed. Predictive dreamers often have drawn disdain from others, most notably the Old Testament's most famous dreamer, Joseph. His jealous brothers say, "Here comes this dreamer. Come now, let us kill him and throw him into one of the pits; then we shall say that a wild beast has devoured him, and we shall see what become of his dreams" (Genesis 37:19–20).[13] He gains more acceptance as an interpreter, however, when he accurately tells the imprisoned chief cupbearer and Pharaoh's baker what their dreams mean.

A hierarchy of divine messages exists within the Bible, however. "It is as if God is one kind of being for Jacob and another kind for Joseph. To Jacob, he speaks directly or in a dream or vision so unequivocal that it requires no interpretation. He never speaks thus to Joseph. The 'Spirit of God' that Pharaoh (not Joseph himself) says is in Joseph is a talent, a gift of God, but not one that requires communication with God for its functioning" (Miles, 1995, 79). Joseph receives his messages, passively and indirectly through symbolic dreams (his own and those he interprets). A prisoner and an outsider to the entire social order in which he exists, Joseph's dream interpretation saves Egypt and gains his acceptance into the community.

A cinematic hierarchy of dreamed messages also exists. Dreams on film reveal more about the dreamer than the interpreter, so people who can interpret their own dreams rank highest on the list of intriguing cinematic dreamers, followed by dreamers who seek interpretations from others. Unlike Joseph's elevated status, outside dream interpreters on film are usually supporting characters rather than stars, relegated to serving as bookwormish shrinks as in *Ordinary People* (1980) or quirky New Age in-laws as in *Stir of Echoes* (1999). Like the outcast prisoner Joseph, however, film characters in *Spellbound* (1945), *Marnie* (1964), *Ordinary People*, *Stigmata* (1999), and *Stir of Echoes* also gain freedom and acceptance through dream interpretation, regardless of the predictive or non-predictive nature of their dreams.

Though less plentiful than in the Old Testament, the New Testament has profound dream episodes that also shape the future. The best-known is probably Joseph's dream about the birth of Christ in which an angel appears with a prophecy in the form of a literal message: "Joseph, son of David, do not fear to take Mary your wife, for that which is conceived in her is of the Holy Spirit.... When Joseph woke from sleep, he did as the angel of the Lord commanded him; he took his wife, but knew her not until she had borne a son; and he called his name Jesus" (Matthew 1:20–25). Similarly, the three wise men, after presenting their gifts of gold, frankincense and myrrh to the baby, leave for their own country by another way upon "being warned in a dream not to return to Herod" (Matthew 2:11–12).

In Joseph's second divine communication, an angel of God warns him in another literal dream: "Rise, take the child and his mother, and flee to Egypt, and remain there till I tell you; for Herod is about to search for the child, to destroy him" (Matthew 2:13). Again Joseph obeys the message in the dream. Later when Herod dies, an angel of the Lord appears in another dream to Joseph in Egypt, saying "Rise, take the child and his mother, and go to the land of Israel, for those who sought the child's life are dead" (Matthew 2:19–21). Joseph follows instructions until he hears that Archelaus reigns over Judea in place of his father Herod. "Being warned in a dream he withdrew to the district of Galilee. And he went and dwelt in a city called Nazareth, that what was spoken by the prophets might be fulfilled" (Matthew 2:22–23). A dream lasting perhaps twenty minutes had effects that altered the destiny of mankind.

Although an admittedly fictionalized account based on the Nikos Kazantzakis novel of the same name, Martin Scorsese's controversial film *The Last Temptation of Christ* (1988) also includes several divine visions and a prophetic dream of biblical proportions that lasts for almost thirty minutes. Interwoven throughout the nearly three-hour epic are tempting visions of lusty snakes, bloody apples, and devilish flames. The film concludes with the last temptation: Christ's dream in which he is offered the chance to come down from the cross and live the rest of his life as a normal man.

In Christ's dream, a girl introduces herself as his guardian angel and says that God has spoken to her of his crucifixion. "Let him die in a dream, but let him live his life." To which Christ replies, "All the pain.... That was real." She answers, "Yes, but there won't be anymore." Later in the dream, the angel is revealed as the devil in disguise. Interestingly, the dream says Christ will die in a dream, but live in real life, but the onscreen action is the exact opposite. Scorsese's inclusion of this lengthy dream sequence is a cinematic test of faith for the film's hero ... and the audience.

Although a firm believer in unfulfilled wishes being expressed in dreams, Freud had no faith in divinely inspired visions and dreams. He writes in *The Interpretation of Dreams* (1994):

> Those writers of antiquity who preceded Aristotle did not regard the dream as a product of the dreaming psyche, but as an inspiration of divine origin, and in ancient times, the two opposing tendencies which we shall find throughout the ages in respect of the evaluation of the dream-life, were already perceptible. The ancients distinguished between the true and valuable dreams which were sent to the dreamer as warnings, or to foretell future events, and the vain, fraudulent and empty dreams, whose object was to misguide him or lead him to destruction [5].

Whether considered divinely predictive or demonically fraudulent, this pre-scientific idea of dreams was in keeping with the general conception of the universe at that time, which was "accustomed to project as an external reality that which possessed reality only in the life of the psyche. Further, it accounted for the main impression made upon the waking life by the morning memory of the dream; for in this memory the dream, as compared with the rest of the psychic content, seems to be something alien, coming, as it were, from another world" (Freud, 1994, 5). Not surprisingly, within the pre-scientific world view, the believed source of a dream, the historic period in which the dream occurs, and the dreamer's relationship with God all influence its predictive interpretation.

On the other hand, Jung — who recounts his personal dreams and visions at length in *Memories, Dreams, Reflections* — believes dreams and visions encompass the entire realm of humanity, rather than merely imaginary fulfillment of suppressed wishes. "Dreams may give expression to ineluctable truths, to philosophical pronouncements, illusions, wild fantasies, memories, plans, anticipations, irrational experiences, even telepathic visions, and heaven knows, what besides" (Jung, 1933, 11). He agrees with Freud that dreams are the voice of the unconscious, but says dreams go beyond defining a neurosis by offering "a prognosis or anticipation of the future and a suggestion as to the course of treatment as well" (6).

In *Dreams* (1974), Jung also differentiates between the prospective function of dreams and their compensatory function. "The latter means that the unconscious, considered as relative to consciousness, adds to the conscious situation all those elements from the previous day which remained subliminal because of repression" or because they were too insignificant to reach consciousness (41). On the other hand, "the prospective function is an anticipation in the unconscious of future conscious achievements, something like a preliminary exercise or sketch ... roughed out in advance" (41). Clearly more of a metaphysician than Freud, Jung also believed that dreams originate in the psyche.

Although dramas and comedies such as *Spellbound* (1945), *Vertigo* (1958), *Marnie* (1964), *Ordinary People* (1980), *The Story of Adele H.* (1975), *Pee-wee's Big Adventure* (1985), *National Lampoon's European Vacation* (1985), and *Analyze This* (1998) portray the unconscious mind as the origin of visions and dreams, the science fiction, fantasy, and horror genres rely almost exclusively on the supernatural, pre-scientific conception of dreams originating from an outside source. In addition, these dreams rarely echo divinely predictive dreams from the Bible; instead they often have religious undertones, but focus mainly on the demonically fraudulent dreams sent by dead people, the devil, and telepathic psychotics.

Visions

In the thriller *Stir of Echoes* (1999), blue collar worker Tom Witzky (Kevin Bacon) is hypnotized by his sister-in-law and then given a post-hypnotic suggestion that "opened a door" in his imagination that allows an everyday, ordinary guy like Tom to experience supernatural phenomena. This open door leads to frightening visions of a dead girl, a suicide attempt, a brutal rape, a threatening neighbor, flashing red lights, and a bloody tooth extraction. Tom's visions (and one predictive dream), apparently generated by the ghost with a grudge, flash back into the murdered girl's past and flash forward into his own future.

Originating from a more benign source though no less frightening are the visions endured by 23-year-old hairdresser Frankie Paige (Patricia Arquette) in *Stigmata* (1999), the creepy tale of a powerless atheist versus the powerful Catholic Church. Channeled through a dead stigmatic priest's stolen rosary beads, Frankie has visions of the crucifixion that are accompanied by real bleeding wounds, a deep voice, and a newfound knowledge of an ancient biblical language. When medical science can find no explanation other than a presumed case of epilepsy, religion enters in the

A post-hypnotic suggestion opens the door to terrifying dreams and visions for ordinary guy Tom Witzky (Kevin Bacon) in *Stir of Echoes* (Artisan Entertainment, 1999). Photograph by Michael P. Weinstein.

form of Vatican investigator Father Kiernan (Gabriel Byrne) who determines the supernatural cause of her visions. During these possessions by the dead priest, Frankie sees bloody images of herself as invisible forces inflict wounds upon her; the visions also predict her future for she will die from these manifested visions unless she is freed of the stigmata.

In addition to the struggle between art and science, *Stigmata* examines the struggle between science and religion. In researching his role as Father Kiernan, Byrne says he saw videos of stigmatics and personally met some of these people.

> Scientists will tell you that stigmatics psychosomatically induce these wounds in themselves—that the power of the mind creates the visions and is strong enough to actually produce blood from the hands, from the side, or from the feet.... It just depends on what your view of the world is, if you believe it's a religious thing then it comes from faith; if you believe in science, then it's psychosomatically induced.[14]

In the three-way cinematic struggle of art, science, and religion in *Stigmata*, art can surely claim the victory.

Prophetic Dreams

Twenty-one-year-old orphan Christine York (Robin Tunney) in *End of Days* (1999) has had prophetic dreams about the devil all her life. "I've seen him before in my dreams—nightmares really," she says to security specialist Jericho (Arnold Schwarzenegger) after encountering the prince of darkness in the form of a man (Gabriel Byrne). "He takes me and makes love to me."

Beginning as his own waking experience, the devil telepathically transmits his thoughts into Christine's dream. In the dream, he has a menage à trois with a mother and daughter as their bodies merge and morph into each other. One of the women turns into Christine, who wakes up screaming for the comfort of her traitorous caretaker. "He came for me again," she cries, adding that this time (December 29, 1999) it felt closer. She is unaware that the devil must conceive a child before the millennium in order to unleash his evil powers on the world.

In Dreams (1998) features more than a dozen of Claire Cooper's (Annette Bening) prophetic dreams about the criminal activities of psychotic killer Vivian Thompson (Robert Downey, Jr.). These dreams are prophetic because they predict the future of important events over which she could have some control to change if she understood the meaning of the dreams. Poor Claire, however, fails to realize the significance of her name and believes that she is reliving the past in her dreams rather than getting a glimpse of the future.

The film also includes one of Vivian's prophetic dreams in which he sees Claire lying dead in a lake. He views her from an underwater point of view then again from above the ground. When Vivian awakens, he tells Claire, "I had a bad dream. My mommy was dead in the water, but she had your face." When she asks if that means he will kill her, Vivian answers, "I hope not." Like Claire, he fails to realize the significance of his prophetic dream and the severity of his psychosis.

Precognitive Dreams

Precognitive dreams, which predict the future of trivial events over which we have no control and are experienced while asleep, are almost as rare as divine dreams on film. Directors avoid precognitive dreams for one obvious reason: If the dream depicts a trivial event, why bother going to the trouble of constructing a predictive dream sequence to represent it? Fortunately some films such as the Joel Coen-directed comedy *Raising*

Arizona (1987) devote themselves exclusively to elevating the trivial to out-
landish heights. In the film a loving though neurotic childless couple, H.I.
and Edwina McDunnough (Nicolas Cage and Holly Hunter), kidnap a
baby boy to call their own. This action prompts an unlikely chain of events
and brings forth a mercenary Neanderthal — a "warthog from hell"— who
tries to steal the baby from them and hold him for ransom.

The night of the kidnapping, H.I. has a precognitive dream in which
he sees this future, but knows it is too late to turn back. He narrates the
dream as it occurs:

> I drifted off thinking about happiness, birth, and new life. But now I was
> haunted by a vision of ... he was horrible. A lone biker of the Apocalypse.
> A man with all the powers of hell at his command. He could turn the day
> into night and lay to waste everything in his path. He was especially hard
> on the little things. He left a scorched earth in his wake.... I don't know if
> he was dream or vision. But I feared that I myself had unleashed him.

Once unleashed, the lone biker is unstoppable, and H.I. has no control over
the ensuing mayhem in his life. In one of his typical understatements, H.I.
observes: "I premonisced [sic] those were the end of the salad days."

Based on the long-running Broadway musical, *Fiddler on the Roof*
(1971) includes an elaborate dream sequence that is fraudulently (though
not demonically) prophetic, i.e., Tevye (Chaim Topol) recounts a horrific
dream to his wife that he never actually experiences. Instead, he concocts
the dream from his imagination, filling it with the couple's dead relatives
rising from their graves to warn of the disasters that will follow the marriage of their eldest daughter to the local butcher. Hoping that his wife
will interpret the dream as prophetic, he relies upon superstition (a message in a dream) and tradition (her beloved grandmother and other lost
relatives) to convince his wife that their daughter should marry the tailor
instead of the butcher.

Shared Visions and Prophecies

So far, the cited visions and predictive dreams on film have been experienced by a single character (and then vicariously experienced by millions
of others). What about shared dreams? In *Our Dreaming Mind* (1994),
dream researcher Robert L. Van De Castle says based on lab experiments
and his own personal experience with dream telepathy, "The dream-to-
dream or unconscious-to-unconscious connection may carry a more powerful charge than an agent's conscious attention" (433). Yet he also

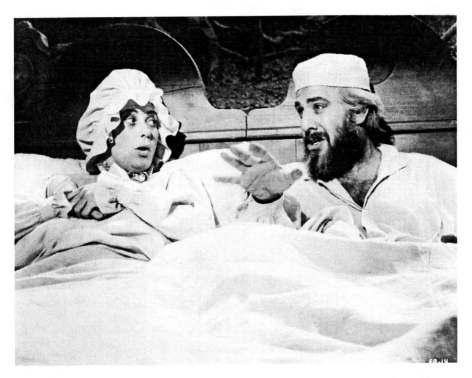

Tevye (Chaim Topol) recounts a fraudulently prophetic dream to his wife (Norma Crane) that is enacted in the background behind the bed in *Fiddler on the Roof* (United Artists Corporation, 1971).

acknowledges that the field of parapsychology and its application to paranormal dreaming generates ongoing conflicts. "Many scientists think that science would be thrown into a state of chaos if the findings which seem to be at such marked variance with how the real world supposedly works, were accepted" (412). The film world thrives on this state of chaos, however.

As every film connoisseur knows, when more than one character has the same vision or dream, it always comes true — regardless of its seemingly chaotic elements. Christine and Jericho share the same grisly vision in *End of Days*, proving that his alcoholism and her assumed mental illness are not causing hallucinations. All the above-ground dwellers in *The Time Machine* (2002) share the same dream of what lies underneath the planet. The inhabitants of *Dark City* (1997) not only share the same dream, but actually live it. Two psychically linked teens (whom nobody believes) share dreams about an evil being called The Tall Man in *Phantasm II* (1988). Likewise, four disregarded high school students share nightmares about a hideously disfigured child killer named Freddy Krueger in *A Nightmare on Elm Street* (1984). In the film, religion (symbolized by a crucifix that keeps falling off the wall) and science (represented by a high-tech sleep laboratory that can provide no answers) are ineffective in providing psychic protection against Freddy — the only way to fight him is through lucid dreaming, i.e, self-awareness during a dream and the ability to consciously alter the content of the dream to suit the dreamer's purposes.

On the lighter side, not all shared visions and dreams on film predict something evil. In *Dreamscape* (1984), Alex Gardner (Dennis Quaid) and Dr. Jane DeVries (Kate Capshaw) share an erotic adventure on a train when he dream-links with her. This exact sequence — including the dreamed ticket taker — is actualized at the film's conclusion. In *Field of Dreams* (1989) based on W.P. Kinsella's novel *Shoeless Joe*, a baseball fanatic (Kevin Costner) and his wife (Amy Madigan) have the same dream. Because they share this ancient power of prophecy, hearing the mysterious voice proclaiming "If you build it, he will come" and spending the family's entire savings on a baseball diamond in the middle of an obscure corn field in Iowa suddenly do not seem so ridiculous— at least to them.

Chapter 11

Dreams as Wish Fulfillment

During a live performance at Madison Square Garden during the *No Strings Attached 'N Sync World Tour 2000*, frontman for the popular boy band Justin Timberlake told the crowd: "I think I can speak on behalf of all five of us when I say that we never, ever in our wildest dreams ever imagined that it was gonna go this far."[15] Timberlake's announcement was not merely telling thousands of screaming pubescent girls what they wanted to hear, he was perpetuating the century-old Freudian theory of dreams as wish fulfillment.

In *The Interpretation of Dreams* (1994), Freud defines all dreams as wish fulfillment, whether simple wish fulfillment (getting what we want), counter-wish-dreams (getting the opposite of what we want), or anxiety dreams (seemingly evoking fear or terror instead of simple wish fulfillment). Freud's complicated theory can be summarized by this brief scene from the James Bond movie *Goldfinger* (1964): Beautiful actress Honor Blackman strolls over to Bond, a.k.a. Secret Agent 007 (Sean Connery) and murmurs: "My name is Pussy Galore."

"I must be dreaming," he replies in amazement. Although Bond obviously is not dreaming, he perceives the situation as fulfillment of his most fervent wishes, or as Freud notes, "in colloquial language the dream is predominantly the gracious fulfiller of wishes. 'I should never have imagined that in my wildest dreams,' we exclaim in delight if we find that the reality surpasses our expectations" (Freud, 1994, 43). The reality of Ms. Galore is a combination of a lovely face, perfect body, and provocative name that surpass even Bond's expectations for the ideal woman.

In keeping with Freud's theory that wishes also may be disguised by dream distortion (or censorship), lusty Agent 007 soon discovers that Ms. Galore's inner qualities—she willingly works as the pilot for Goldfinger, an evil international gold smuggler and cold-blooded killer—do not match her outer beauty. Her physical appearance disguises the ugliness within.

Freud writes, "In the sexual constitution of many persons there is a masochistic component, which has arisen through the conversion of the aggressive, sadistic component into its opposite… It is obvious that such persons may have counter-wish-dreams and disagreeable dreams, yet these are for them nothing more than wish-fulfillments, which satisfy their masochistic inclinations" (66).

Based on Bond's chosen profession and his penchant for seducing the bad guys' girlfriends, he is not without masochistic inclinations. Even his name implies a sadomasochistic struggle between the bonds of his employment, which require a duty to his country, and his bondage to lust, which keeps him an involuntary slave to his insatiable sexual desires. However, whether simple wish fulfillment or counter-wish-dream, James Bond meeting Pussy Galore is a figurative dream come true for him.

Freud also describes the anxiety dream as wish fulfillment, although Bond clearly does not belong in this category. Possessing good looks, expensive suits, high-tech gadgetry, sports cars, and an arsenal of weapons likely relieves any nervousness he may feel when encountering women. "Neurotic anxiety has its origin in the sexual life, and corresponds to a libido which has been deflected from its object and has found no employment" (Freud, 1994, 69). Because Bond's libido is rarely deflected from its object and usually enjoys full-time employment, his figurative wish fulfillment dream fails to meet Freud's criteria for anxiety.

Dream Studies

Modern dream researchers and sleep scientists generally disagree with Freud regarding all dreams as wish fulfillment. In his recent study of the psychology and physiology of dreaming, sleep expert Ernest Hartmann writes, "Dreams are obviously meaningful in the sense of dealing with our emotional concerns; they are not random products of a disordered brain. I cannot agree with Freud, however, that every dream can be best understood as the fulfillment of a wish" (Hartmann, 2000, 67). His main objection to Freud's theory is that wish fulfillment is too limited a definition for the limitless content of dreams. "Fulfilling a wish may be one way of picturing (contextualizing) an emotional concern, but certainly not the only way" (71).

Hartmann cites a well-known study of patients' dreams when they are thirsty and when they are not. The results show that the thirsty condition prompts dreams of drinking water, which can be considered wish fulfillment, but also inspires dreams of feeling thirsty, feeling scratchy, feeling irritable, and looking for something to drink, which do not indicate wish fulfillment (71). Based on these and numerous other studies, Hartmann concludes that instead of wish fulfillment, dream content is a mixture of physiological and psychological functioning. "Dreaming is better than waking at making connections: it makes connections more broadly in the nets of the mind, and they are guided by the dominant emotions of the dreamer. The dream contextualizes the emotion or emotional concern of the dreamer" (72).

In *From the Kekule Riddle: A Challenge for Chemists and Psychologists* (1993), Wynn Schwartz of Harvard Medical School writes about the results of the Dream Study Group of the Boston Psychoanalytic Society and Institute in 1992, which investigated relationships between waking concerns and the content of dreams.

> In our exploration of various questions that involve information processing during REM sleep, we have viewed dream content as personally significant in its manifest form as a more or less direct representation of the dreamer's problems and concerns. We have also assumed that symbolization, metaphor, and the like, when they appear in the manifest dream story, show attempts at integrating the problems into other concerns that also matter to the dreamer. Our focus on the meaningfulness of the manifest dream is in partial contrast to the traditional Freudian view that the dream is essentially the disguised representation of a childhood wish (Freud 1900) and in opposition to the position that dream content is essentially the result of nearly random neocortical activity driven by the pons (Hobson 1988). We believe that dreams are meaningful constructions [281].

The study suggests that rather than a wish finding fulfillment through a dream, a problem finds a solution through a dream.

Schwartz says that problems identified through pre-sleep interviews reappear in the following night's dreams. "Over and over, we found that the problems we identified during the pre-sleep interview were clearly represented in the dreams although the dream representations might be in the form of an obvious metaphor, symbol and the like" (281). He notes that a link also exists between the effects dreams have on the ability to later solve these problems. His team looked at whether the problems represented in the dreams showed modifications suggesting that sleep made problems more workable than in pre-sleep. "We viewed metaphor as more useful than literal representation since we thought metaphor was an attempt to integrate different thoughts together, showing more 'working through.' We wanted to see if successful dream solutions translated to more effective solutions the next day and we found this to be the case"

(281). The study also indicates that successful problem resolution is most often preceded by metaphorical representation in dreams.

Jung disagreed with the wish fulfillment theory long before Hartmann and Schwartz, however. In *Dreams* (1974), he criticizes Freud's concept of the wish-fulfilling and sleep-preserving function of dreams as too narrow, instead focusing on the significance of sleeping and dreaming to conscious life. "Dreams, I maintain, are compensatory to the conscious situation of the moment" (38). He sees the conscious and unconscious life hanging in a delicate balance. "As against Freud's view that the dream is essentially a wish-fulfillment, I hold ... that the dream is a *spontaneous self-portrayal, in symbolic form, of the actual situation in the unconscious*" (49). Jung's emphasis on the mythology and spirituality of the dreaming life also sets his views apart from those of Freud.

Making connections, solving problems, and spontaneous self-portrayal of the unconscious sometimes find their way into filmed dream sequences, but usually within the Freudian context of dreams as wish fulfillment.

Making Connections

Hartmann's theory that dreaming "is better than waking at making connections" because the dream "contextualizes the emotion or emotional concern of the dreamer" becomes evident as the Neil Jordan horror film *The Company of Wolves* (1984) progresses. The story offers a sexy retelling of Little Red Riding Hood contained within the framework of an adolescent girl's dreams of wish fulfillment. Angry at her older sister, Rosaleen (Sarah Patterson) locks herself in her toy-filled room and smears her face with makeup (presumably not her own) in an attempt to appear more mature. Despite her sister's repeated banging on the door and a brewing storm outside the open window, Rosaleen falls into a disturbed slumber in which she dreams of herself as a strong, independent, and highly desirable version of Little Red Riding Hood traipsing through the dangerous wolf-infested forest to visit her grandmother.

Her angry waking emotions manifest themselves through the dreamed death of her sister by a pack of wolves, and her adolescent insecurity is resolved through Rosaleen's dreamed rejection of a lustful village boy who relentlessly pursues her. Despite waking warnings about boys and sex, the red-cloaked dream Rosaleen enthusiastically climbs a large phallic structure, an enormous tree with a nest full of eggs, a tin of red lipstick, a hand mirror, and a coiled snake hissing at her from a nearby branch. Carole

An adolescent girl (Sarah Patterson) dreams that she is Little Red Riding Hood on her way to visit Granny when she encounters a handsome wolfman (David Warner) ready to fulfill her every desire in *The Company of Wolves* (ITC Entertainment, 1984).

Zucker writes in *Film Quarterly* about *The Company of Wolves*, "The sequence is laden with significance, but perhaps most unmistakable, and most important is the resemblance to the tree of knowledge. There are the archetypal images of loss, innocence, and entry into the world of experience" (2000, 68–69). Rosaleen's waking wishes for revenge against her sister, male admiration of her beauty, and first-hand knowledge of sex connect with her dreams of fulfillment.

In her final dream, Rosaleen is willingly devoured by the handsome wolfman and turns into a wolf herself. This wish fulfillment dream, and the dreams leading up to the climactic scene, contain rich Freudian symbols of sex and death that correspond to her entrance into adulthood. Zucker describes Rosaleen's figurative awakening as a point of no return. "Rosaleen's lipstick is likened to the blood on the wolf's mouth, yet the wolf poses no apparent danger for the young girl. While a tear is shed for her loss of childhood, Rosaleen's entrance into the erotic — the emergence of appetite (she like the wolf, can be a predator; she wants the giant phallus, not a mere lad), the masturbatory stroking of her lips with moist fingers, the specter of childbirth ... do not provoke — in the context of the dream world — fear or anxiety" (69).

Through her wish fulfillment dreams, Rosaleen makes connections with her waking life and satisfies her need for a more mature personal and sexual identity. For the audience, her wish fulfillment dreams satisfy our need for experiencing the adrenaline rush that accompanies danger without actually endangering ourselves.

Solving Problems

Unlike *The Company of Wolves*, which uses dreams as a framework for the story, *Analyze This* (1998) includes specific wish fulfillment dreams to solve the problems of the general story. In this Harold Ramis-directed comedy, Paul Vitti (Robert De Niro) is a mob boss troubled by nightmares and panic attacks. Although he seeks help from Dr. Ben Sobel (Billy Crystal), a psychiatrist, he refuses to undergo therapy because it conflicts with his tough-guy persona, and therefore he continues to manifest symptoms. Consistent with Schwartz's findings that "problems we identified during the pre-sleep interview were clearly represented in the dreams although the dream representations might be in the form of an obvious metaphor, symbol and the like," the film relies on dreams — rather than on-going therapy — to solve Vitti's problems. A tough mobster may not want to share intimate secrets with his doctor, but sharing dreams in which his weaknesses are disguised through the mixed-up metaphors of dreams is far less threatening.

Secretly suffering from a guilty conscience because his mobster father was murdered in front of him and he did nothing to stop the attack, Vitti dreams that he hears a baby crying. When he goes to the refrigerator for milk he sees that the milk is black. Not knowing about the murder, Dr. Sobel incorrectly concludes from the dream that Vitti has a guilty conscience about wanting to kill his father and make love to his mother. Furiously denying any Oedipal instincts, Vitti asks, "Have you ever seen my mother?" Later in the film, Dr. Sobel tells him that Freud believed all the characters in a dream were representations of the dreamer. Therefore, the child receiving the black milk (or improper nourishment) and the careless parent supplying it are aspects of Vitti's own personality.

Although his first attempt at dream interpretation misses the mark, Sobel tries again with his own dream in which he is walking with Vitti and then gets shot. With tears streaming down his face, Vitti kneels over him crying, "Papa, Papa." Based on his dream, Dr. Sobel realizes that the classically

Freudian fears expressed through Vitti's symptoms are caused by conflicts about death, not sex. The characters in *Analyze This* use dreams to solve Vitti's mid-life crisis and subsequent desire to leave the "family business." Vitti's dream also satisfies his wish to be punished; Dr. Sobel's dream satisfies his wish to help Vitti resolve his Oedipal conflict. Because Vitti's dream is merely described, but Dr. Sobel's dream is shown, the audience instantly perceives the greater importance of Dr. Sobel's dream and its interpretation.

Spontaneous Self-Portrayal

Jung's theory of dreams as "spontaneous self-portrayal" in symbolic form is grotesquely brought to life in *The Mask* (1994), a comedy originally conceived as a horror film by its director, Chuck Russell, who also directed *A Nightmare on Elm Street 3: Dream Warriors* (1987) (Craddock, 2001). When nerdy bank clerk Stanley (Jim Carrey) finds a mask that gives its wearer magical powers during the nighttime, he awakens the next morning and believes he dreamed the strange events from the preceding evening. The mask turns the soft-spoken clerk into an over-the-top playboy. Stanley explains how the mask works: "It's like it brings your innermost desires to life. If deep down inside you're a little repressed and a hopeless romantic, you become some sort of a love-crazy wild man." Neither the repressed bank clerk nor the cartoonish love god represent a genuine self-portrayal of Stanley, however.

While the mask acts as an artificial waking fulfiller of wishes, Stanley's dream provides genuine wish fulfillment while he is asleep. During the evening of the dream, he is denied admittance to the Coco Bongo night club where his unrequited love interest, Tina Carlyle (Cameron Diaz), works as a performer. His trousers get splashed by a passing car and the valet brings his borrowed jalopy to the curb as Tina approaches. Rejected, soaked, and humiliated, Stanley relives the experience in his dream, but this time his wishes are fulfilled. He is a cool, confident, well-dressed version of himself, who draws heavily on his cigarette, knows the right things to say, and drives a white convertible Porsche.

As Tina approaches him in the dream, she leans over his right ear and licks the side of his face. This unexpected occurrence exemplifies Freud's theory of a "dream of convenience," a subcategory of wish fulfillment in which an actual bodily need or physical sensation is incorporated into the dream as a means of preserving sleep (Freud, 1994, 34). In this case, Stanley's slobbering dog, Milo, eventually wakes his master when the physical sensation becomes too intense and sleep can no longer be preserved.

The real Stanley is glimpsed for only a few minutes during the dream sequence, a spontaneous self-portrayal of the man he longs to become. As the film ends and he gets the girl (Tina finally dumps her thuggish boyfriend), Stanley and the audience realize his potential for actualizing his wish fulfillment dream of being cool, confident, and well-dressed.

Similarly, in Tom DiCillo's independent sleeper *Living in Oblivion* (1994), movie director Nick Reve (Steve Buscemi) loses his temper during a film shoot in which everything goes wrong. Delayed by actors who forget lines, cameramen who cannot focus, and unsteady boom operators, filming stops completely when a mysterious beeping ruins the scene. After Nick viciously insults his cast and crew, he frantically searches for the source of the noisy distraction. He wakes from his anxiety dream and turns off the beeping alarm clock. Previously unaware that he was dreaming (as were we), Nick incorporates the physical sensation — in this case ringing ears caused by a beeping alarm clock — into the dramatic story of his dream.

The ticking clock in Lara's dream in *Lara Croft: Tomb Raider*, based on a popular video game, uses the same concept of a dream of convenience. While a real clock begins ticking in her home, an imaginary clock begins ticking in her dream. In the dream, her father explains that the clock holds the key to the All-Seeing Eye, which in turn will help her activate a magic time-stopping machine that will save the world. As the ticking in the dream intensifies, so does her desire to wake and find the clock hidden by her father within the walls of her mansion. What the film lacks in logic, it makes up for in convenience.

In keeping with Freudian theory, most dreams on film provide wish fulfillment for their characters and the films themselves provide wish fulfillment for the audience. Returning briefly to the theory of film as a public dream, Glen O. Gabbard writes in his essay, *The Psychoanalyst at the Movies*, that "just as dreams function as wish-fulfillments (at least in many cases), so do films provide wish-fulfilling solutions to human dilemmas" (1997, 431). Unlike dreams that enter our psyche each night with indiscriminate images and unbidden ideas, we pick our favorite genre and choose individual films based on our particular needs for wish fulfillment, whether it be a two-hour adventure as a handsome secret agent, a ruthless criminal reflecting on his life, an ordinary person with newfound supernatural abilities, or any of countless escapist scenarios.

All The Pretty Horses (2000), based on the national bestseller of the same name by Cormac McCarthy, is a modern western about a young Texas ranch-hand who runs away to Mexico to become a real cowboy. After the recent divorce of his parents and death of his grandfather, and threatened with the impending loss of his job on the ranch, John Grady Cole (Matt Damon) rides off with his best friend to seek a new life elsewhere. Kind, compassionate, honest, fair, and brave, he fulfills the wishes of every audience member who has ever longed to escape from a small town, a dead end job, or a dysfunctional family.

Just when John Grady is on the brink of living his dream with a rewarding job, a girlfriend, Alejandra (Penelope Cruz), and respect from his peers, he is unjustly thrown into a brutal Mexican penitentiary. While incarcerated, he has wish-fulfilling dreams in which he remembers his brief taste of freedom and success: He rides pretty horses and makes love to a pretty girl. Director Billy Bob Thornton does not share John Grady's dreams with us as the character fulfills his wishes (and ours) by escaping a constricting environment; the dream sequences first appear when his plans are thwarted and his life no longer reflects his (or our) fulfillment of wishes.

The dream sequences in the film are quite brief compared to the lengthy dream references and descriptions in McCarthy's book, which emphasize the aggressive, rather than sexual, instincts of the character

A young cowboy (Matt Damon) has wish fulfillment dreams of pretty horses and a pretty girl (Penelope Cruz) while locked in a Mexican prison in *All the Pretty Horses* (Miramax Films, 2000). Photograph by Van Redin.

Matt Damon (left) and Henry Thomas with director Billy Bob Thornton (right) on location for *All the Pretty Horses*. Thornton worried that the dream sequences made his western too contemporary (Miramax Films, 2000). Photograph by Vann Redin.

while dreaming. For instance, on his first night in prison, John Grady has this dream:

> That night he dreamt of horses in a field on a high plain where the spring rains had brought up the grass and the wildflowers out of the ground and the flowers ran all blue and yellow far as the eye could see and in the dream he was among the horses running and in the dream he himself could run with the horses and they coursed the young mares and fillies over the plain where their rich bay and their rich chestnut colors shone in the sun and the young colts ran with their dams and trampled down the flowers in a haze of pollen that hung in the sun like powdered gold and they ran he and the horses out along the high mesas where the ground resounded under their running hooves and they flowed and changed and ran and their manes and tails blew off of them like spume and there was nothing else at all in that high world and they moved all of them in a resonance that was like a music among them and they were none of them afraid horse nor colt nor mare and they ran in that resonance which is the world itself and which cannot be spoken but only praised [McCarthy, 1992, 161].

Although Thornton has said he would not cave in to pressures of making his western more commercial, he admits the dream sequences "may seem more contemporary, but otherwise I wanted it to be like a John Ford western."[16] He need not have worried about seeming too contemporary. Freud described the instincts represented by wish fulfillment dreams more than one hundred years ago.

Chapter 12

Dream Themes: Sex and Death

In *A Nightmare on Elm Street* (1984) teenaged Nancy Thompson (Heather Langenkamp) is most at risk from dead disfigured child killer Freddy Krueger (Robert Englund) in her dreams. When she falls asleep in the bathtub — despite repeated warnings from her mother not to do this — and Freddy's razor-clawed fingers reach up from the water between her open legs, does Nancy dream of sex or death? In *Sleeping, Dreaming, and Dying* (1997), sex, death, and sleeping are linked as voluntary actions that unite us in a pool of shared images and memories. "The willingness to lose our sense of self that allows us to sink into sleep or orgasmic fusion can also allow us to be unafraid of dying. We might say that sleeping and orgasm are sublimated forms of dying" (The Dalai Lama, 49). Young, repressed, and frightened, Nancy likely dreams of sex *and* death.

Overtly Jungian views of sex, however, are not very popular in today's cinema. Jung downplays the significance of sexual dreams by explaining them as either residue from the day or compensatory functions that make up for a disappointing sex life. He writes in *Dreams* (1974) "The sexual language of dreams is not always to be interpreted in a concretistic way — that is, in fact, an archaic language which naturally uses all the analogies readiest to hand without their necessarily coinciding with a real sexual content" (Jung, 49). Declaring that sexy dreams are not really sexy dreams, but rather representations of archaic symbols unrelated to sex altogether, does not provide a particularly effective marketing strategy for increasing box office totals.

Basic Instincts

Dreams of sex and death generate far more interest in most moviegoers, particularly the target audience of young men who see *A Nightmare*

On Elm Street and its sequels at the theater and then watch these movies again at home on videotape like recurrent nightmares. Rather than linking these two themes universally in the many shared images of the collective unconscious, Freud views dreams of sex and death as unconscious individual expressions of our two most basic instincts. He tentatively sets forth in *The Ego and the Id* published in 1923, that two classes of instincts exist: the sexual instinct or Eros, which comprises uninhibited sexual urges and the self-preservative instinct for life; and the death instinct, which, supported by theory and biology, is represented by sadism and urges to lead organic life back into the inanimate state (Freud, 1989).

Six years later, in *Civilization and Its Discontents*, Freud says he firmly concludes based on biological parallels that in addition to "the instinct to preserve living substance and to join it into even larger units, there must exist another, contrary instinct seeking to dissolve those units and to bring them back to their primaeval, inorganic state. That is to say, as well as Eros there was an instinct of death" (1961, 77). Contemporary critics of Freud say his ideas about sex are merely a reflection of the repressed Victorian era in which he lived. Yet the instincts for sex and death revealed through dreams — and contained within the overall framework of Freudian wish fulfillment — remain vibrantly alive in recent dreams on film, despite a few inconsistencies with modern science.

Owen Flanagan writes in *Dreaming Souls* (2000) that according to recent studies, adults rarely dream about sex. "Erotic feelings are relatively uncommon in dreams, after adolescence. Sexual acts are also uncommon. As few as 6 percent of adult dreams involve feelings of eroticism or sexual activity" (149).

Yet erotic feelings and sexual acts occur quite frequently in cinematic dreams — especially young female cinematic dreams tinged with the element of fear. In his book, *The Age of Television* (1982) Martin Esslin suggests that we have come to expect a certain level of sexual intimacy from characters viewed on a screen. "The people we view in close-ups on the television screen appear to be as near to us as our sexual partners during an embrace. And yet they are glimpsed behind a glass screen, through a window that cannot be opened.... The world it shows us on its stage, behind that window through which we can see but cannot grasp or touch, is essentially a world of fantasy" (32). Although Esslin refers specifically to television, the same concept applies to the cinema. Viewing a sexual dream on film allows us to experience someone else's erotic secrets without having to divulge our own.

Although many horror films, fantasies, and sci-fi thrillers feature dream sequences with explicit sex, sometimes erotic symbols and innuendos are employed for this purpose. In *The Company of Wolves* (1984), an adolescent girl dreams of being pursued by an ardent male admirer, climbs a tall phallic tree, and (despite warnings from adults) allows herself to be devoured by the big bad wolf waiting for her in the forest (see Chapter 11). In *Picnic at Hanging Rock* (1975), the entire film appears to be an adolescent girl's dream about being pursued by an ardent male admirer, climbing a huge phallic rock structure, and (despite warnings from adults) allowing herself to be lost forever inside the mysteries of the rock.

In *Dreamscape* (1984), Dr. Jane DeVries (Kate Capshaw) clearly explores her erotic feelings and engages in sexual acts with psychic dream-linker Alex Gardner (Dennis Quaid) during a shared dream onboard a speeding train. Fully dressed in soft white clothes as warm sunlight streaks in through the windows, they take the time to explore each other's bodies during their first time together, a skillful blending of romanticism and lust. Although in the dream Dr. DeVries is a willing partner, in her waking life she is afraid of involvement because she does not want to be just another of Alex's many conquests and fears an intimate relationship with him will jeopardize the important dream-linking project at the sleep lab where they work.

Sex with the Devil

Other sexual dreams on film contain less symbolism and eroticism, relying instead on graphic depictions of sex and an escalated sense of fear for titillating audience members. In *End of Days* (1999), twenty-one-year-old Christine York (Robin Tunney) has experienced recurring nightmares since childhood in which she has violent sex with the devil (Gabriel Byrne). These dreams are sent by Satan to prepare her for his arrival on December 31, 1999, when he can rule heaven and hell by impregnating Christine by the stroke of midnight.

These dreams are crucial for plot development for they — and some surrealistic visions — increase in intensity and frequency as the date draws near. Although the dreams are discussed throughout the film, only one dream sequence shares Christine's nightmares with the audience. The scene begins with the devil's reality of having sex with a mother and daughter simultaneously, then transforms into Christine's nightmare of sex with Satan.

Byrne says that while shooting the scene it did not feel like a dream sequence. "The thing about dreams is that they feel real so you can't act being in a dream. You act real being in a dream." He says the reality factor is what troubles Tunney's character the most. "Part of the conflict with the idea of having sex with the devil is that during her waking hours this is something she cannot contemplate, but in a dreamlike sequence, it's OK to do it. Our sexual dreams—who we are as sexual beings—may be a little frightening to actually contemplate in reality."[17]

Luckily, with the help of her protector Jericho (Arnold Schwarzenegger), Christine's dreams remain mere fantasies and the prince of darkness never consummates his plan to impregnate Christine with his child and take over the universe.

In a similar scenario, sweet young Rosemary (Mia Farrow) in *Rosemary's Baby* (1968) dreams she is raped by a hairy beast as weird onlookers chant and perform ritualistic activities. As her bizarre pregnancy—wrought with strange, excruciating pains and cravings for raw meat—nears its inevitable conclusion, Rosemary wonders whether the devil fathered her child. Adapted from Ira Levin's best-selling novel, the terror of *Rosemary's Baby* is derived from the powerful combination and manipulation of our sex and death instincts. These instincts are revealed in a "dream" (actually a real event occurring during a drug-induced stupor) which starts by preserving life and joining into a larger unit (making love with her husband) and ends with the destruction of Rosemary's previous life and representation of sadism (raped by the devil, formerly kind, innocent, and religious Rosemary is now the mother of the Antichrist).

Dreams of sex with the devil also were common stories in medieval folklore, yet these dreams actually have a scientific basis. Stories of supernatural nocturnal encounters with evil beings usually begin with the appearance of a strange creature who manages to paralyze terrified victims before sexually assaulting them. A male visitor is called incubus; a female visitor assaulting a male is succubus. Stories of supernatural sex and nocturnal visitors have a common root which says they may be products of vivid hypnagogic (associated with sleep onset) hallucinations (Dement and Vaughan, 1999). "Vivid hallucinations, behaviors, and terror are all fascinating symptoms of some of the sleep disorders that blur the line between sleep and wakefulness. People with narcolepsy, sleepwalking, night terrors, sleeptalking, and REM disorder can get stranded in sleep's borderlands, where everyday rules of thought and behavior don't seem to apply" (Dement and Vaughan, 1999, 195). Most people have experienced simple hypnagogic images or sensations upon falling asleep.

The most common type of hypnagogic experiences are isolated images or feelings that float through our consciousness, like having our skin lightly touched. Other commonly reported sensations include the sudden feeling of falling, which leads to a startle and jerk of the limbs. "More frightening, but completely normal, are hypnagogic images like a bright flash of light, or sounds such as a loud bang that seems to come from inside the head. These images and sensations are almost always fleeting, and because the sleeper is not yet deeply asleep, they often cause a return to full wakefulness" (Dement and Vaughan, 1999, 195).

Dement compares these simple hypnagogic hallucinations with truly vivid hypnagogic hallucinations which occur when someone falls instantly into REM sleep without going through the intervening non–REM sleep stages first. "When REM sleep occurs so quickly, the dream story often begins exactly where wakefulness ended and is a seamless stream of consciousness from the real world to the dream world. Occasionally this can happen to normal individuals if they are extremely sleep deprived, or after waking up later in the sleep cycle, when REM is favored" (196).

Hypnagogic hallucinations are frequently associated with patients who suffer from the sleep disorder narcolepsy. "What we don't know is why the content of these vivid hypnagogic hallucinations is so often very unpleasant or downright terrifying.... Most often there is a pervasive fear, sometimes so strong that people are sure they are about to die. Other parts of their hallucination, which may include people, animals, parts of objects, or just shapes, have a mysteriously nightmarish quality" (196).

In addition to scientific explanations of vivid hypnagogic hallucinations, some modern dreams of sex with the devil (or demonic creatures) still retain the supernatural element from centuries ago. A recent study by Ventura, California-based Barna Research Group, a marketing research firm, explored diversity of beliefs across the country and found that twenty-seven percent of Americans polled have a strong belief that Satan is real, with Mormons being the most likely to accept Satan as more than merely a symbol of evil. Researchers reported that fifty-nine percent of members of the Church of Jesus Christ of Latter Day Saints think Satan is real, while about one-fifth of Catholics, Episcopalians, and Methodists share this belief.[18] Belief in the devil is not a prerequisite to finding demonic images on film frightening, however.

Had Dr. King (Charles Fleischer) at the Katja Institute for the Study of Sleep Disorders in *A Nightmare on Elm Street* been more concerned with sleep science and less concerned with supernatural "body hocus pocus," he may have diagnosed Nancy with narcolepsy (the muscular paralysis of REM that occurs while awake), REM behavior disorder (muscles that should be paralyzed during REM but are not, resulting in the body acting out the dreams of the mind), or some other sleep disturbance. After all, she falls instantly into REM sleep while bathing, sitting in class, and at home after pumping herself full of over-the-counter stimulants and a pot of coffee (conveniently hidden under her bed). She also screams for help and fights Freddy in her sleep.

A better doctor may have diagnosed Nancy more scientifically, but he or she still would have been wrong: How can science possibly explain a psychopathic child murderer—burned to death by neighborhood vigilantes—who somehow manages to wear razor-clawed gloves to slice and dice teenagers in their dreams and has the ability to intrude upon their waking lives as well? The answer cannot be found in science or art, but in a blending of the two.

Although on the surface Nancy dreams of her death instincts, the deeper subtext of the dreams and of the film itself (and, of course, the seemingly endless string of sequels) surrounds her suppressed feelings of sexuality, in many ways similar to the adolescent girls in *The Company of Wolves* and *Picnic at Hanging Rock.* Nancy and her three teenaged friends represent two young couples at a sexual crossroads. One of the couples is sexually active; Nancy and her boyfriend, Glen (Johnny Depp), are celibate, though not from a lack of trying on his part. "Morality sucks," Glen laments while the other couple has sex down the hall and he sleeps alone. Even in her dreams, Nancy remains pristine. Although her sleazy friend, Tina (Amanda Wyss), traipses through her nightmares with Freddy wearing a see-through nightie, virginal Nancy plods through her dreams in conservative pajamas.

Freddy sharpens his knives and noisily scrapes his claws before attacking his young victims. In keeping with Freudian dream symbolism, "anything long and straight could thus be interpreted to signify a male sexual organ, and almost any open receptacle could represent a female sexual organ. Gushing water in a dream landscape was seen as an orgasm. Even stabbing someone with a knife was interpreted as aggressive sexual activity" (Lewis, 1995, 215). Although the victims are physically lying in bed when they are slashed to death, mentally they are lured into Freddy's abandoned boiler room, his home before the vigilantes seek revenge by torching the place. A boiler, of course, is a storage tank for hot liquid.

After two of the teens are murdered in their sleep and Freddy prepares to kill Glen, too, he calls Nancy on her unplugged telephone and says enticingly, "I'm your boyfriend now, Nancy!" Repulsed and attracted to the fiend—as she is to her sexual urges—Nancy plunges into a dream with the intent of bringing Freddy out of the dream world and into her waking life so her police-chief father can arrest him.

In her 1999 essay, "Touring the Dream Factory: The Dream-Film Connection in *The Wizard of Oz* and *A Nightmare on Elm Street*," Kelly Bulkeley writes that *Nightmare's* moral message is that an evil will never

completely die, a lesson which resonates among the target audience of adolescent males who enjoy ritualistic viewings of the movie about teenagers alternately suppressing and releasing their sexual and aggressive instincts.

They identify not simply with Nancy and her teenage friends, but with Freddy Krueger himself. For adolescent boys, Freddy expressed all the terribly urgent sexual desires they feel rising up within themselves. The *Nightmare on Elm Street* movies are brutally honest about how frightening these desires can be, stimulating fears and fantasies of violent fragmentation, death, and destru-

Alive in the nightmares of teenagers, knife-wielding serial killer Freddy Krueger (Robert Englund) symbolizes repressed instincts of sex and death in *A Nightmare on Elm Street* (New Line Cinema, 1984).

tion. By watching these horror movies again and again, in small, furtive, emphatically *non*-family gatherings, adolescent boys seem to find a measure of comfort in sharing their inner experiences of trying to come to terms with the Freddy Krueger within each of them [Bulkeley, 1999, 107].

Near the end of the film, Nancy remembers Glen's earlier advice (based on what he says is the Balinese method of dreamskills): "If you create a monster in your dreams, turn your back on it and take away its energy so it will disappear." Nancy literally makes an attempt to take away Freddy's power and figuratively attempts to take away the power of her repressed sexuality by turning her back on the "monster" she has created. The film's ending, which brings her dead friends and mother back to life on a clear sunny day, ends on a terrifying note that Freddy is not powerless after all. No amount of repression can fully "kill the monster," i.e., subdue her intense adolescent sexual urges and Freddy's desire to kill.

Death Dreams

Since ancient times, people have feared death dreams as something supernatural. The Greek philosopher Heraclitus (born around 540 B.C.) writes: "A man in the night kindles a light for himself when his sight is extinguished; living he touches the dead when asleep" (Cohen, Curd, Reeve, 1995, 27, frag.23). Even today, one of the most popular myths about dreaming is that if you die in a dream, you actually die. "I don't know how this idea became part of our cultural beliefs about dreams," writes psychotherapist Joan Mazza in *Dreaming Your Real Self* (1998). "If someone dreamed of his death and then died in the dream, how would anyone else know?" (34). Despite this lapse in logic, *A Nightmare on Elm Street* and other thrillers including *Dreamscape* (1984) rely on the audience's suspension of disbelief regarding dreams about death actually killing the dreamer.

In *The Cell* (2000), child psychologist Catherine Deame (Jennifer Lopez) must enter the mind of a comatose serial killer, Carl Stargher (Vincent D'Onofrio), in order to help his latest victim, a young woman trapped in a cell slowly filling with water. Although an old pro at dream-linking through high-tech machinery in the sleep laboratory where she works, Catherine is warned to press the touch-sensitive microchip implanted in her hand if she feels too threatened by the dream images. The doctor who works with her explains the situation to the FBI detective, Peter Novak (Vince Vaughn): "If she came to believe that Stargher's world is real then theoretically her mind could convince her body that anything that was done to it there was actually done. Like the old wive's tale if you die in your dream, you die in real life." When Catherine does confuse the dream with reality, Peter enters a three-way dream-link to save her.

A scientific explanation for dying in one's sleep has nothing to do with razor-clawed psychos, dream-linking assassins, or serial killers who trap women in cells then lapse into comas.

> Apnea is an unrecognized killer, but is hiding in plain sight. Every night more than 50 million Americans stop breathing. In a stunning evolutionary failure, nature endowed us with throats that tend to collapse during sleep and stop air flow but did not endow our sleeping brains with the ability

> to start breathing again calmly. At this breathless moment, the immediate
> future holds only two possibilities: death or waking up to breathe [Dement
> and Vaughan, 1999, 168].

Our throats serve the multiple functions of breathing, talking, eating, and
drinking, which all have individual engineering requirements. For the
most efficient breathing during sleep, we should have "a stiff tube that
could not collapse while we suck air into the lungs" (172). Dying in one's
sleep from purely physical causes such as apnea likely has been attributed
to supernatural causes such as dreams about dying over countless generations.

The Approach of Death

In *The Dream Encyclopedia* (1995), James R. Lewis cites a study in
which four age groups— 21–34, 35–49, 50–64, and 65 and over — were
questioned about their dreams. According to the study, subjects in the
21–34 and 50–64 groups reported having more dreams than the other two
groups. "Contentwise, the most dramatic finding was a direct correlation
between age and frequency of dreams about death and dying. Dream content also changes among the retired (especially the institutionalized)
elderly, who often experience dreams about lack of resources. Finally,
dreams among those who are dying often include the theme of life after
death" (Lewis, 5–6).

Bearing some resemblance to the results of actual sleep studies, *Wild
Strawberries* (1957) depicts the troubled dreams of a 78-year-old professor of medicine. During the final hours before receiving an honorary degree
at Lund Cathedral for his fifty-year career, Dr. Isak Borg (Victor Sjostrom)
endures a frightening series of flashbacks and dreams that recount his fail-
ures throughout his life. Accused of being an egoist by those around him
because of his cold rigidity, he secretly tells himself that the faculty "should
have made me honorary idiot," indicating a self-awareness that is echoed
in his dreams.

In addition to dreaming of confronting his own lifeless body falling
out of a coffin (see Chapter 3), he also dreams of seeing his childhood
sweetheart again — Sara (Bibi Andersson) who broke up with him years
ago to marry his brother. They sit together outside in a strawberry patch.
Although she is now 75 and he 78, in the dream she is the beautiful young
girl he loved in the past while he remains the old man of the present. She
holds up a mirror in front of him and demands, "Have you looked in the

mirror, Isak? Then I'll show you what you look like. You're a worried old man who's soon going to die."

The dream then cuts to the confused doctor seeking entry to a building where he will be tested by an examination board for his medical abilities. Led by a somber examiner, he arrives in a classroom with a dispassionate jury of ten people, who will help determine his fate. Unable to see anything in the microscope except the reflection of his own eye and incapable of answering the questions correctly, Dr. Borg cannot even tell if a patient is alive or dead, nor remember a doctor's first duty. The examiner informs him: "A doctor's first duty is to ask for forgiveness." Dr. Borg is accused of guilt by his late wife and found incompetent in his profession. "You are also accused of minor offences: callousness, selfishness, ruthlessness," the examiner tells the miserable old man.

Near the end of this lengthy three-part dream sequence, Dr. Borg is led by the examiner to the woods where they witness a reenactment of his wife's passionate love affair with another man, a scene that helped harden his heart years earlier. Near the end of his life, Dr. Borg's dreams reflect not only his fear of death, but his fear of dying a failure.

In *Papillon* (1973), based on the autobiographical writings of French thief Henri Charriere, the same fears trouble a character in a different situation. Falsely imprisoned for life for the murder of a pimp in 1930s France, Papillon (Steve McQueen) repeatedly risks his life in attempts to escape. Sentenced to two years in solitary confinement (his punishment for escaping), his rations are temporarily cut in half because he refuses to betray a fellow inmate, and he resorts to eating cockroaches. Sick and starving, his body wastes away, his teeth rot, and his clothes hang in filthy tatters over his pasty flesh. During this low point, he dreams about his life and impending death in two vivid dreams.

In the first dream, Papillon walks outside in the sand wearing expensive leather shoes. Suddenly he sees a judge in a bright red cape standing in front of a seated jury of 12 people dressed in black. The judge shouts at Papillon:

"You know the charge."

"I'm innocent," Papillon says. "I didn't kill that pimp. You couldn't get anything on me and you framed me."

"That's quite true, but your real crime has nothing to do with a pimp's death," the judge bellows.

"Well, then. What is it?"

"Yours is the most terrible crime a human being can commit. I accuse you of a wasted life."

"Guilty," Papillon says softly.

1957

SUEDE

DRAME

LES FRAISES SAUVAGES
SMULTRONSTALLET

REALISATEUR
Ingmar Bergman

"The penalty for that is death."

"Guilty ... guilty ... guilty," Papillion acknowledges sadly as he walks away. Although Papillon's wretched life in prison is nothing like the pampered existence of Dr. Borg, they both fear the ultimate judgment: a death that follows a meaningless life.

Sentenced to death in his first dream, Papillion then experiences a second dream that exacts the penalty. The scene opens with Papillon and fellow inmate (Dustin Hoffman) riding in a car cheered on by crowds and a band. The music stops with a freeze frame on the car. The next scene begins with a freeze frame in the prison yard. Dressed in street clothes, Papillon sees two prisoners who were killed earlier, now alive and waiting for him. He runs in silent slow motion down a tree-lined path. The camera turns sideways, then upside down. As he approaches, the men and Papillon have pale skin and black-rimmed eyes. He realizes they are not alive; it is he who is dead. He says in slow, garbled speech: "You're dead." In this wish fulfillment dream, Papillon gets the ultimate punishment he feels he deserves.

Dreams of death are usually the result of severe stress about life's conditions (e.g., feelings of inadequacy) or the actual approach of death (e.g., old age or starvation). While providing important insight into a film character's psyche, death dreams can be frightening and uncomfortable to watch — making them especially popular in horror, sci-fi, and edgy art film genres (unlike sex dreams which are included in all genres). "Sleeping, dreaming and dying are 'ego's shadow zones,' where Western science is often ill at ease, far from its familiar territory of the physical universe or physiological causality" (The Dalai Lama, 1997, 1).

Although general audiences may be more familiar and comfortable watching depictions of sexual instincts than death instincts in dream sequences, these two basic motivations in life — as outlined by Freud — often appear simultaneously in soul-searching dreams and terrifying nightmares on film.

Opposite: In this French film card for *Wild Strawberries,* an elderly professor of medicine (Victor Sjostrom) and his daughter-in-law (Ingrid Thulin) meet three hitchhiking teenagers (top) who inadvertently cause him to have painful flashbacks and dreams about his wasted youth and lost love (middle photos and bottom left). The group stops for a meal before the final leg of the journey (bottom right) (Svensk Filmindustri, 1957).

Chapter 13

Nightmares

Clairvoyant Claire Cooper (Annette Bening) escapes from a mental hospital to seek the psycho who is transmitting dreams to her in the Neil Jordan thriller *In Dreams* (1998). "What's this?" a confused hospital employee asks Claire's roommate upon finding her empty bed. The roommate answers "her dream, your nightmare." However, the situation can just as easily be described as "her nightmare, your dream," because Claire remains plagued by nightmares, and the hospital staff believes her mental images are hallucinatory constructs of her imagination. In short, a nightmare is in the mind of the beholder because one character's nightmare of sex and death may be another character's dream of simple wish fulfillment.

Three Types of Nightmares

What constitutes a nightmare? In the late 1960s sleep scientists did studies for 150 nights on the REM and NREM nightmares of thirty-seven subjects with a history of nightmares. They determined that spontaneous awakenings with varying degrees of anxiety occur in all stages of sleep (Fisher, et al., 1970). Based on results of this study, the research team concluded that three types of nightmares exist: *stage four arousal nightmare* (not really a dream, this is a NREM state of confusion or hallucination often accompanied by a scream and increased heart rate); *REM anxiety dreams* (frightening images occurring in the mind after about twenty minutes of REM sleep with little or no accompanying response in the central nervous system; i.e., controlled anxiety); and *stage two nightmares* (intermediate dreams that fall between stage four and REM anxiety, with moderate anxiety, cardiorespiratory response, and nightmarish content). Stage two nightmares usually are associated with a single frightening scene, such as falling or choking that develops simultaneously with a vocalization.

"The manifest content of many REM nightmares appears as threatening as some of the stage 4 nightmares, but the degree of fright and the concomitant physiological response is very much less" in REM nightmares (Fisher et al., 1970, 187).

Nightmares on film usually depict (what scientists would classify as) stage two nightmares, which offer the most "dramatic" dreams containing the physiological responses of NREM sleep and the psychological complexities associated with REM mentation. The supposedly REM anxiety dreams shown in films—terrifying images accompanied by physiological responses such as mumbling, tossing, turning, thrashing, crying, and shouting, would actually indicate a stage four arousal nightmare, which technically is not a dream, but "a pathological formation that occurs in a postarousal stage in which the subject may be hallucinating and somnambulistic [sleepwalking]. Its severity is determined by certain physiological conditions, e.g., deeper stage 4 sleep promoting ego regression, dissolution of controls and defenses, and eruption of intense traumatic anxiety" (Fisher et al., 1970, 185). Nightmares in films such as *The Company of Wolves* (1984), which combines terrifying images in a storylike structure consistent with REM mentation and physiological responses of stage four arousal, exemplify the dramatic appeal of taking scientific liberties with dream depiction.

In *The Interpretation of Dreams* (1900), Freud quotes studies that determined fifty-eight percent of dreams are unpleasant or disagreeable and only about twenty-nine percent are pleasant (1994, 45). According to Mark Blagrove, vice president of the Association of the Study of Dreams and co-author of a report issued at the 2000 International Conference for the Association for the Study of Dreams in Washington, a recent study concurs with this hundred-year-old research. "Nightmares and other bad dreams can be caused by negative waking emotions, such as stress, anxiety, fear and sadness" and specific traumatic experiences "such as divorce or surgery, can also lead to more frequent nightmares."[19] Participants in the study were rated on the frequency that they could recall their past dreams, with an average of 2.4 dreams per week. Results indicate that dreams are more responsive to negative emotions and challenges, rather than mirroring the full range of human emotions. Dreams on films also reflect more upon the negative, with nightmares overwhelmingly appearing more often than pleasant dreams.

Several studies concluded that Americans have been suffering from insomnia and post-traumatic nightmares since the terrorist attacks on September 11, 2001. "We are entering a national epidemic of nightmares," accompanied by "scenes of destruction, feelings of vulnerability, and anxieties over the future [which] ... have entered our psyches and are surfacing in our dreams in an unprecedented manner" (Conklin, 2001, E4). CNN and other network news programs similarly reported that sales of sleep aids and anti-anxiety drugs have skyrocketed since the attacks. Although we certainly dream about a variety of situations, the post-traumatic nightmares are what we tend to remember upon awakening.

The scientific and artistic constitution of these nightmares is not quite the same, however. Although filmic nightmares encompass a limitless range of subject matter, depictions of sex and death — what Freud calls our basic instincts— usually are interwoven among other nightmarish themes, often involving slow motion or paralysis (an internalization of lost motor control during REM sleep). In addition to disturbing themes, these nightmares can be replayed repeatedly with slight alterations or escalations during recurrent dreams, a popular device for plot development in film. The final element to consider in evaluating cinematic nightmares concerns the emotional effects on the dreamer. Studying the themes, recurrence, and emotional effects of actual and cinematic nightmares gives insight into their popularity with filmmakers and indicates some reasons why nightmares on film deviate from the standards found in scientific studies.

Themes

Nightmares on film usually revolve around themes of vulnerability, insecurity, helplessness, powerlessness, or loss of control. Frightening scenes from a character's waking life are transformed into frightening symbols when he or she dreams. Therefore, a sick old man whose time is running out has a nightmare of a clock with no hands (*Wild Strawberries* [1957]) and a middle-aged woman who hides her emotions dreams of a white mask lying on the ground and the people in her life as actors on a stage (*Another Woman* [1988]). Frightening symbols transformed from everyday emotions maintain scientific accuracy because frightened people do have frightening dreams. "During the day, as the brain's nerve cells are used, they change their behavior. If they have been stimulated, the cells may become more reactive. If you have been frightened during the day, the nerves that control the startle response and feelings of fear will be more reactive that night" (Dement and Vaughan, 1999, 304).

Jung suggests that the opposite might be true as well. In *The Spirit in Man, Art, and Literature* (1966), he says that a dream is like a great work of art because despite its seemingly simplistic style and apparent obviousness, the true theme remains ambiguous. "It presents an image in much the same way as nature allows a plant to grow, and it is up to us to draw conclusions. If a person has a nightmare, it means he is either too much given to fear or too exempt from it; if he dreams of a wise old man, it means he is either too much of a pedant or else in need of a teacher" (Jung, 104).

If we accept the contemporary theory of Dement and the traditional view of Jung, we have an explanation for every nightmare. In *Pee-wee's Big Adventure* (1985) when Pee-wee (Paul Reubens) has nightmares about his stolen bicycle being dipped in boiling oil by a devilish creature, he is reacting to stimulated nerve cells in his brain that were activated during the day as he obsessed about his missing bike. Conversely, when the well-muscled and heavily armed Sarah Conner (Linda Hamilton) in *Terminator 2: Judgment Day* (1991) has a nightmare about the impending nuclear holocaust, we see the hidden fear she has repressed beneath the outward facade of strength.

Sarah's nightmare is especially frightening because it taps into her (and our) vulnerability, insecurity, helplessness, powerlessness, and loss of control in the midst of an unstoppable force of destructive evil. An Academy Award-winner for best visual effects, make-up, and sound effects editing, *Terminator 2: Judgment Day* uses all those crafts in one nightmarish dream sequence. Escaped from a psychiatric hospital, Sarah, with her son, John (Edward Furlong), and a terminator unit sent from the future to protect her (Arnold Schwarzenegger), prepare for an uncertain future in which three billion people may be killed and vicious robots rule the earth. While planning her strategies, Sarah naps on a picnic table in which she has a terrifying dream.

In the nightmare, she walks toward a park in Los Angeles and sees children and mothers playing on the swings and other playground equipment. She sees a younger version of herself with a small child and shakes the noisy chain link fence surrounding the playground as she tries to shout a warning. No sound comes from her mouth and her warnings are ignored. Suddenly, massive explosions followed by raging fires envelope the playground and spread rapidly to surrounding areas. Sarah watches and screams as bodies burn in front of her. People, buildings, buses, and nature burn and melt from catastrophic waves of fire that consume all life.

Unlike most film characters who must contemplate their nightmares and discuss the dream symbols with a friend or counselor, Sarah realizes her nightmare is prophetic, thereby presenting her with options to change the future, but only if she acts immediately. "Dreams that leave the dreamer uncomfortable, fearful, concerned, or anxious, require action. They have a special and unique meaning for the dreamer that, when made conscious, requires action" (Mazza, 1998, 122). Upon awaking, Sarah is fully prepared

Horrific images of explosions, fires, mass destruction, and Terminators plague the dreams (and waking life) of a young single mother in *Terminator 2: Judgment Day*. Pictured are Arnold Schwarzenegger (foreground) as a rewired Terminator and Robert Patrick as the T-1000, the deadliest Terminator of them all (Universal Studios Florida, 1996).

to battle whatever forces stand in her way of stopping the mass destruction. The frightening dream themes strengthen her resolve that we can make our own fate.

Recurrence

The most frightening aspect of nightmares on film (and of actual nightmares) is their tendency to recur. "A nightmare whose problem is not addressed, can turn into a recurrent nightmare. Or a recurrent dream may escalate to become more and more nightmarish in the unfolding of the dream images and outcome" (Mazza, 1998, 122). Recurring nightmares are not restricted to "Elm Street," but haunt characters in all kinds of films through hundreds of different symbolic forms, while still relying on the overriding theme of fear.

Since ancient times, recurring dreams were viewed as more important than single dreams. In the Old Testament, Joseph's dreams and other people's dreams that he interprets are all prophetic and symbolic. In the Joseph stories, the dreams occur in pairs, likely to enforce their importance and command the dreamer's attention. "The possibility of an idle dream was recognized by the ancients. From the literature of the ancient Near East we have accounts of double, triple, and even sevenfold repetition of dreams in which one symbol is successfully substituted for another, although the basic meaning and central theme remain the same throughout the series" (Sarna, 1989, 257).

Thus, Joseph's prophetic dreams about his brothers' sheaves bowing down to his and the other dream in which the sun, the moon and eleven stars bow to him are essentially the same. In addition to his father's obvious preference for Joseph, his egocentric dreams may well have pushed his brothers over the edge, turning his recurrent dreams of unaddressed problems into nightmares. As they plan their attack, the brothers say to each other, "Here comes this dreamer. Come now, let us kill him and throw him into one of the pits; then we shall say that a wild beast has devoured him, and we shall see what become of his dreams" (Genesis 37:19–20).

Recurrent nightmares also intrigued the great philosophers and psychiatrists of earlier generations. French philosopher Blaise Pascal writes of recurrent dreams in a collection of his work, published posthumously in 1670. "If we dreamed every night the same thing, it would affect us as much as the objects that we see every day.... But because the dreams are all different, and even the same one takes various forms, what we see in dreams affects us much less than what we see when awake because of the continuity ... for life is a dream a little less swiftly moving" (Pascal, 1965, 27, frag. 52). The lack of continuity in remembered dreams may well have an impact on how these nightly messages are (or are not) incorporated into a daily routine. A random nightmare may not be cause for alarm, but recurrent nightmares with the same theme establish their own form of continuity that deeply affect the dreamer.

While Freud never officially revised the 1900 publication of *The Interpretation of Dreams*, he returned to it many times over the years, adding discussion and notes. In a 1920 essay, he addresses one single exception to the idea of dream as wish fulfillment: repeated dreams of a trauma are not considered wish fulfillment, but are attempts to establish dominance over the trauma so the pleasure principle can begin.

Likewise, Jung also attributed great meaning to recurring dreams.

"An obscure dream, taken by itself, can rarely be interpreted with any certainty, so that I attach little importance to the interpretation of single dreams. With a series of dreams we can have more confidence in our interpretations, for the later dreams correct the mistakes we have made in handling those that went before" (Jung, 1933, 14). Acknowledging the importance of recurring dreams also acknowledges the importance of their origin.

A traumatic event or even the fear of its recurrence is the usual cause of nightmares. "If the event was very upsetting, the nightmares of the images of the calamity might continue for years, with the nightmares being one of several symptoms of posttraumatic stress disorder (PTSD). The nightmares may become a personal metaphor for stress, terror, or threats of all kinds, just as any recurring dream can act as a repeating metaphor" (Mazza, 1998, 121). Filmmakers commonly use repeating metaphors even without dream sequences. Recurring nightmares merely supply a convenient means of portraying the repetition of symbolic forms of fear surrounding a particular theme, usually future events such as the murders in *In Dreams* (1998) and impregnation by the devil in *End of Days* (1999), or a past trauma like the boating accident in *Ordinary People* (1980) and a witch hunt in *Sleepy Hollow* (1999).

In *The Talented Mr. Ripley* (1999), a remake of the 1960 film *Purple Noon,* emotionally unstable Tom Ripley (Matt Damon) suffers from recurrent nightmares. The contents of these nightmares is not revealed; we see only their disturbing effects on Tom as he sleeps. Whether he dreams of past traumas when he killed people or future events when he will kill again remains a mystery. The nightmares seem to be Tom's single source of fear and vulnerability. When his new homosexual lover starts asking him to reveal secrets and share the cause of his nightmares, Tom responds by strangling his boyfriend to death during a presumed embrace.

Emotional Effects

In addition to theme and recurrence, the emotional effect on the dreamer helps differentiate a dream from a nightmare. A disturbing dream that is only disturbing while we sleep does not qualify for nightmare status. True nightmares seem alarmingly real, place the dreamer in the most vulnerable situations, and linger for hours, days, weeks or even years afterwards. Ben Rock, production designer of *The Blair Witch Project* (1999), says the pseudo documentary about three young filmmakers lost in a haunted woods shows nightmarish imagery presented as reality. "You wake up from a dream and say, 'Thank God, that was just a dream.' In the case of *Blair Witch*, you see things as they happened because the film presents a nightmare as real. In your nightmares, the Blair Witch would come out and eat your head; in the movie, it doesn't work like that."[20] The most frightening dream elements that create the most devastating emotional effects are not revealed on camera, but in our own imaginations.

Romantic poet Samuel Taylor Coleridge captures the emotional effects of recurrent nightmares in "Ode to the Departing Year," originally published in 1796.

> The voice had ceas'd, the vision fled;
> Yet still I gasp'd and reel'd with dread.
> And ever, when the dream of night
> Renews the phantom to my sight,
> Cold sweat-drops gather on my limbs;
> My ears throb hot; my eye-balls start;
> My brain with horrid tumult swims;
> Wild is the tempest of my heart;
> And my thick and struggling breath
> Imitates the toil of death!
> [Coleridge, 1995, 518].

Audiences are far more likely to see artistic manifestations of cold sweat drops, throbbing ears, swimming brains, and thick struggling breath in depictions of filmic nightmares than scientific signs of increased heart rate, nocturnal penile tumescence, hyperpolarizing signals sent to the spinal cord resulting in REM paralysis, and stimulated nerve cells in the brain. The emotional effects of nightmares link the audience to the character because we have all felt similar fear.

Although occasionally even tough guys like Doug Quaid (Arnold Schwarzenegger) in *Total Recall* (1990) have recurrent nightmares that effect them emotionally, the usual victims of filmic nightmares are children. Research suggests that when children "approach the age of six or seven, their ability to communicate and the comfort they receive enable them to accept nightmares as 'just a bad dream'" (Lewis, 1995, 174). In general, even small children do not seem overly concerned with frightening dreams. "Nightmares are part of the normal pattern of childhood development. We know that most children have 'bad dreams' and will begin to report them as soon as they are able to express their feelings and experiences" (Mazza, 1998, 123).

Freud writes that the dreams of little children are often simple fulfillments of wishes, and, therefore, uninteresting compared to adult dreams. Children's dreams "present no problem to be solved, but they are invaluable as affording proof that the dream, in its inmost essence, is the fulfillment of a wish" (Freud, 1994, 38). Children's nightmares on film, however, can be enormously interesting, as evidenced by a boy's recurring nightmares of a snakeman monster in *Dreamscape* (1984), a girl's recurring nightmares of a disabled boy and an evil father in *Paperhouse* (1989), and a boy's recurring nightmares of (and possession by) a supernatural force of evil in the form of Freddy Krueger who stalks the son of the actress who battled the razor-clawed fiend in her earlier *"Nightmare"* movies in *Wes Craven's New Nightmare* (1994). "Those dreams that convey into our sleep the many painful emotions of life, these are also anxiety-dreams, in which this most terrible of all the painful emotions torments us until we wake. Now it is precisely by these anxiety-dreams that children are so often haunted" (Freud, 1994, 45). Their perceived vulnerability, innocence, lack of adequate verbalization skills, and inability to distinguish reality from illusion make children highly sympathetic victims of filmic nightmares.

Despite the many similarities between actual and filmic nightmares, one important difference exists: Filmmakers usually apply the same standards when representing the nightmares of children as they do with adults. Jung writes in *Dreams* (1974) that a "child's dream is different from an adult's, just as the dream of an educated man differs from that of an illiterate. There is something individual in the dream: it is in agreement with the psychological disposition of the subject"(4). Although films tend to show variations in how adults and children react to their nightmares, the dreams themselves are virtually the same.

Consider these dreams from a family of four (father, mother, teenaged son and daughter) in *National Lampoon's European Vacation* (1985). Due to a mixup on a television game show, the Clark W. Griswold family wins an all-expenses-paid trip to Europe. While en route, they relax on the plane and three of them experience dreams of wish fulfillment while one has a nightmare. Teenage angst cannot be distinguished from middle-aged angst. One family member dreams of dancing at a swanky night club; another dreams of mountain climbing with the family; another dreams of meeting England's royal family; and the fourth family member has a nightmare about overeating until a hideously bloated stomach forces buttons to pop off the shirt. To whom do the dreams belong?

Actually, teenaged son Rusty (Jason Lively) dreams of the disco; father Clark (Chevy Chase) dreams of the mountains; mother Ellen (Beverly D'Angelo) dreams of meeting Prince Charles and Lady Diana; and teenaged daughter Audrey (Dana Hill) has the nightmare about overeating. Obsessed with her new boyfriend, she fears (with just cause) that he will find someone thinner to date while she travels to Europe. In her nightmare, she is seated alone at a large dining room table as a half dozen uniformed servants bring her steaming plates of food and chilled rich pastries. Accompanied by frenzied instrumental music, the dream is fast and furious, with Audrey stuffing herself with food until her torso puffs up into a ball and pops the buttons off her straining shirt. She wakes muttering "no" and smacking her lips unpleasantly.

Audrey's fears know no particular demographic; any member of her family could have had the same dream. The theme of unrestrained hunger and morbid obesity reflects waking preoccupations that could be shared by anyone, and the smartly dressed waiters and elaborately prepared dishes present a mature appreciation of food. The emotional effect of the dream — waking up with a feeling of self-disgust — also could be felt by any of the other family members — or anyone outside the family.

A frightening series of nightmares with the theme of fear, frequent recurrence (she has endured the same dreams since childhood), and debilitating emotional effects (she is a frigid kleptomaniac) lies at the core of the Alfred Hitchcock thriller *Marnie* (1964). A recurring dream sequence, shown in part and also described by the terrified dreamer, Marnie (Tippi Hedren), relies on classically Freudian elements to interpret the nightmares. The emotionally scarred woman has been traumatized by a violent and sexual childhood that she has successfully repressed, except in her dreams. With the help of her dream-interpreting husband, Mark Rutland (Sean Connery), Marnie heals her inner child from the fear and hatred that are ruining her life.

Early in the film, we see Marnie sleeping in bed at her childhood home muttering in her sleep: "No I don't want to, Mama. Don't make me move, Mama. It's too cold." As she speaks, the camera reveals a male fist banging on the window, and a flash of red. Marnie awakens and sees her mother standing at the bedroom door. She says to her mother, "I was having that old dream again. First the tapping. It's always when you come to the door. That's when the cold starts." Her mother ignores Marnie's dreams.

Later, while sleeping in Mark's home, Marnie's dream reveals itself in more detail. Scary music is followed by tapping, then a flash of red. An impatient male fist taps on the window. Marnie is seen in bed as the camera pans to the window. "Mama. Oh, Mama, don't cry," she says. The room is in the old wooden house where she grew up, but as the camera pans around the room, it dissolves into her bedroom at the Rutland home. "Don't cry, Mama," she says again. Marnie is half-awake, but cannot tell Rutland from her dream at first. He picks up her sleeping pills from the

Much to his dismay, Mark Rutland (Sean Connery) in *Marnie* learns on his wedding night that kleptomaniac, somniloquist wife Marnie (Tippi Hedren) also is frigid (Universal Pictures Company, 1964).

nightstand. Rutland asks about the dream and says he knows she has had it before. Marnie then describes the dream, "First there are the three taps. Then she says 'Get up, Marnie. You have to get up now.' But I don't want to … if I get up I'll be cold and they'll hurt her… I hear the noises and I'm cold."

We can despise Marnie's theft and deceit, and be flabbergasted by her repulsion to the attractive character played by Sean Connery, but we must sympathize with anyone who has recurrent nightmares based on a childhood trauma.

> Although we may be fascinated by the character who accidentally commits a murder, we do not necessarily identify with him. But when we discover that his murdering was a dream, we become more identified with him through our own half-perceived dreamlike impulses to violence. Hitchcock's use of psychiatry in various films has similarly been criticized… Whatever falsification of actual psychoanalytic methods one might object to in such films, the symbolic point, the way in which Hitchcock has

absorbed psychiatry into his aesthetics, remains clear. He uses external intellectual systems with the pure opportunism of the true artist [Braudy, 1977, 53].

Indeed, the artistry of nightmares on film, i.e., portraits of characters' most deeply hidden fears, are presented in a moving picture gallery that lets the audience decide whether it is "her dream, your nightmare" or "her nightmare, your dream" through identification with the character and analysis of dream elements.

Chapter 14

Dream Elements

Clichéd elements of dreams on film include visual and aural/verbal cues that use artistic means to separate dream sequences from the rest of the film. Visual cues such as fade to black, ripple dissolves, sepia tones, slow motion, fluctuating points of view, black and white, the color red, extreme close-ups of an eye, smoke/fog, masks, clowns, dwarfs, mutants, zombies, apples, and mirrors often indicate a character is in an altered state of mind. Aural/verbal cues include garbled sound, discordant tones, circus music, echoes, heartbeats/clocks ticking, and the dreamer saying, "I must be dreaming," none of which bear much resemblance to actual dreams. Dreams on film do not usually feel real because of these cues; our own nightly REM mentation — which likely contains no smoke, dwarfs, mirrors, or ticking clocks — seems genuine, logical, and true while we are experiencing it.

The sci-fi extravaganza *Total Recall* (1990) combines several visual cues (and a musical punctuation) throughout the film to keep the audience unsure of whether Doug Quaid (Arnold Schwarzenegger) is dreaming or awake. The Mars setting glows red in the background as radiation-exposed mutants and a dwarf prostitute fight for their rebel cause through the smoke and explosions. Instead of mirrors, director Paul Verhoeven creates two other reflective images of Quaid to keep us off balance: a holographic Quaid enters dangerous situations before the real one does, and a videotaped Houser (also Arnold Schwarzenegger) tells Quaid he needs to kill him to reclaim his body. The final words in the film portray Quaid and his love interest Melina (Rachel Ticotin), embracing outside. "I can't believe it," says Melina. "It's like a dream….What's wrong?"

"I just had a terrible thought," answers Quaid. "What if this is a dream?"

"Well, then kiss me quick before you wake up."

Filmmakers, actors, and audiences eventually may grow tired of these overused elements if *Living in Oblivion* (1994), a low-budget spoof of low-

Bad guy Richter (Michael Ironside) threatens to shoot Thumbelina (Debbie Lee Carrington) as mutant Tony (Dean Norris) rushes to her aid in the dream-like reality of *Total Recall* (Tri-Star Pictures, 1990).

budget filmmaking, is any indication. In the movie, director Nick Reve (Steve Buscemi) attempts to direct a dream sequence using a cranky dwarf named Tito (Peter Dinklage), an actress whose main credential is having filmed a shower scene with Richard Gere, and an outdated smoke machine that his crew cannot operate. During off-camera scenes within the movie, the star, Nicole (Catherine Keener), repeatedly calls Tito by the name Toto (Dorothy's dog in *The Wizard of Oz* [1939]), an unsubtle allusion to the earlier movie's lengthy dream sequence about a land inhabited by munchkins.

In filming the dream sequence within the film, Nicole stands alone in a smoke-filled red room wearing a bridal gown as Tito enters through a blue door with clouds painted on it. He is dressed like a bridegroom and carries an apple. The sequence, accompanied by eerie circus-type music, represents the woman's anxiety dream about getting married; Tito symbolizes the anxiety. After several unsuccessful takes, Nick confronts the difficult actor.

"Look Tito," he says, "it's not that big of a deal. It's a dream. Strange things happen in a dream. All I want you to do is laugh. Why is that such a problem for you?"

"Why does it have to be a dwarf?" Tito asks.

"What?"

"Why does my character have to be a dwarf?"

"It doesn't have to be a dwarf," Nick replies.

"Then why is he? Is that the only way you can make this a dream — put a dwarf in it? Have you ever had a dream with a dwarf in it? Do you know *anyone* who's ever had a dream with a dwarf in it? NO! *I* don't even have dreams with dwarfs in them. The only place I've seen dwarfs in dreams is in stupid movies like this. Oh make it weird, put a dwarf in it — everyone will go woo, woo, woo, it must be a fucking dream, there's a fucking dwarf in it. Well, I'm sick of it. You can take this dream sequence and shove it up your ass." The character of Tito and the writer-director of *Living in Oblivion,* Tom DiCillo, are fighting an old battle against clichés established in the 1920s, when the Surrealists transformed Freud's psychoanalytic theories into filmed entertainment.

Strange incongruities serve as important symbols for Freud's free association principle adapted for the Surrealist movement in art. Surrealist cinema explores pathological conditions such as nightmares, hysteria, and obsessions, with an emphasis on altered states of consciousness. "Freud's theory of the unconscious, his preoccupation with dreams as a mirror of existence with its own language, and his emphasis on sexual symbolism were to exert a profound effect on these filmmakers" (Giannetti, 1976, 391). Surrealist cinema stressed disorientation and dislocation, making these films the ideal medium for "conveying the weird precision of dreams" (392). During the following years, the figurative logic of symbolization became secondary to a more literal logic of representation in the cinema, enhanced by developments in special effects techniques and computer-generated images. Films with dream sequences, however, retain traces of the Surrealist movement where incongruous and illogical images, such as eyeballs sliced with scissors in the Hitchcock thriller *Spellbound* (1945), or a monkey flying through a dentist's office with a propeller head in the Hitchcock-inspired French thriller *With a Friend Like Harry* (2000), and dwarf bridegrooms holding apples, contain their own dream logic.

Opposite: In this French film card for *Living in Oblivion,* an independent film crew prepares the set for a dream sequence (top left). Within a dream within a film within a film, actors Nicole (Catherine Keener) and Chad (James LeGros) rehearse a scene (top right) and the director (Steve Buscemi), star (LeGros) and cinematographer (Dermot Mulroney) (right center) express their disapproval. The emotional cinematographer (Mulroney) loses his cool on the set within Nicole's dream (bottom) (Entertainment/JDI/Lemon Sky, 1994).

1994

U.S.A.

COMÉDIE

ÇA TOURNE À MANHATTAN
LIVING IN OBLIVION

RÉALISATEUR
Tom DiCillo

UNE COMÉDIE NEW-YORKAISE

Dream Logic

The incongruous, illogical language of dreams has a scientific basis. REM dreams contain detailed scenarios often in contrast to the laws of nature, but fully in keeping with the nature of dream logic. Studies indicate that REM dream reports involve "much more vivid and elaborate imagery, more emotionality, more physical activity, and they are more distorted and implausible; whereas the fragmentary reports usually obtained from non–REM awakenings are much more like loose conceptual thinking about contemporary events" (Snyder, 1970, 127). In *Dreaming Souls* (2000), Owen Flanagan describes REM dreams as "more bizarre than NREM dreams, more akin to watching a Fellini motion picture while high on marijuana than reading the tip about tomato planting in the morning paper while drinking orange juice" (13). Most scientists now believe the psychotic nature of REM dreams emanates from physical rather than psychological causes, as Freud originally theorized.

Because of this physiological leveler, dreams of psychopathic child killers Freddy Krueger (*A Nightmare on Elm Street* [1984]) or Vivian Thompson (*In Dreams* [1998]) would contain no more psychotic elements than the dreams of bumbling food additive specialist Clark W. Griswold (*National Lampoon's European Vacation* [1985]). "A single dream of a psychotic is indistinguishable from the dreams of so-called normal persons. Perhaps the difficulty here is mainly with language and common distinctions" (Mazza, 1998, 120).

Pulitzer Prize-winning biologist Edward O. Wilson describes dreams as the reorganization and editing of information in the brain's memory banks, an overriding physiological process that ignores psychological disturbances. During sleep, when most sensory input has stopped, "the conscious brain is activated internally by impulses originating in the brain stem…. But lacking moment-by-moment input of sensory information, including stimuli generated by body motion, it remains unconnected to external reality. Therefore, it does the best it can: It creates fantasy" (Wilson, 1998, 75).

The level of REM fantasy is sometimes measured on an IUD (incongruity, uncertainty, and discontinuity) scale to determine bizarreness for various characteristics: mismatches in logic regarding time, space or people; unknown or unspecified dream elements that would aid in interpretation; and abnormal shifts in places, people, time, or action. Dement observes that dreams "are very good at melding paradoxical elements, an essential element of the creative process," but also notes that "the act of creation requires an interpretation by waking consciousness" (Dement and Vaughan, 1999, 320). Therefore, a dream seemingly high on the IUD scale makes sense after applying Freud's secondary revision just before awakening or upon awakening, i.e., filling in the missing pieces and finding words to express the visually inexpressible.

Similarly, a film makes more sense when we analyze the details afterwards. Psychological sense or emotional truth, however, may be experienced during the dream or film. "Cinematic techniques appropriating free association or primary process may make a specific visual montage more psychologically true to the viewer" (Gabbard, 1997 432). In *Snow Dogs* (2002) for example, Cuba Gooding, Jr., plays a Miami dentist who unexpectedly inherits a snow-dog team in Alaska. As a middle-aged adult and head of a dental team called Hot Smile, he first learns that he was adopted as a baby. He then dreams of himself as a baby, but with his adult head attached during a frightening dream that reflects the child still remaining within the man. Later, after visiting his deceased mother's residence in Alaska and being abandoned by the racing dogs in a disastrous mushing incident, he dreams that instead of being hurt and lost in the snow, he is back on the beach in Miami and the snow dogs are reclining in lounge chairs talking to him. Although the good dentist is psychologically sound, his dreams would seem to indicate otherwise.

As in the talking-raptor dream in *Jurassic Park III* (see Chapter 15), this dream depicts the struggle to understand (and therefore dominate) nature; indeed, the natural world has a logic and intelligence of its own often beyond our understanding. Yet, the psychological truth and emotional accuracy of these untruthful and inaccurate images remains the driving force behind dream sequences.

Visual and Aural Effects

Visual and aural effects immediately enhance the psychological truth of a dream sequence by touching our emotions. Scott Crowell, director, writer, producer, and star of the psychological thriller *Stranger* (2000), says he used a variety of low-budget effects to enhance his first independent feature. "In the dream and flashback sequences in *Stranger*, I gave them a soft diffused look with a slight tint in order to make these scenes look different from what was taking place in the present. I also added echoed sounds for a dreamlike quality that indicated it wasn't here and now; it wasn't real."[21] These sequences allow us to experience some degree of compassion and understanding for the decidedly unlikeable stranger.

Although Freud maintained that dreams are primarily visual and only

In *Snow Dogs*, talking dogs who wear sunglasses and sip sodas in their lounge chairs on the beach seem perfectly natural according to dream logic (Disney Enterprises, Inc., 2002). Photograph by Doug Curran.

secondarily verbal, most filmed dream sequences include a variety of sound effects to enhance the dreamlike quality of the scene. Echoes and sound distortion represent a few popular devices for punctuating dreams symbolically in conjunction with the dramatic content of the film. Nightmares in *Marnie* (1964) are accompanied by tapping at the window; erotic dreams in *Belle de Jour* (1967) are signaled by ringing bells; dreams in *Cries and Whispers* (1972) are preceded by clock chimes; a heart beats throughout a nightmare in *Wild Strawberries* (1957) and during an erotic dream in *Keeping the Faith* (1999).

In his novel *Heart of Darkness* (1995), Joseph Conrad makes an interesting observation about the words in dreams. "They were common everyday words, — the familiar, vague sounds exchanged on every waking day of life. But what of that? They had behind them, to my mind, the terrific suggestiveness of words heard in dreams, of phrases spoken in nightmares" (Conrad, 1995, 107). Words in dreams — and in dream sequences — are much the same as everyday words. Pronunciation, grammar, and syntax remain the same in dream conversations; what changes is the symbolic content of the words that suggests a deeper meaning.

Although music rarely plays a part in actual dreams, filmed dream sequences rarely appear without it. The frantic music in Audrey's nightmare in *National Lampoon's European Vacation* (1985), the Latin music in

Scottie's nightmare in *Vertigo* (1958), composer Danny Elfman's frightening circus music behind the two dreams in *Pee-wee's Big Adventure* (1985), and the distorted music in *In Dreams* nightmares all set the tone for the dream within the framework of the film. Combined with the images, sounds, and words, music in cinematic dreams produces a dreamlike atmosphere that is unlike our actual dreams, yet lends emotional truth to the scene.

In the comedy *Dudley Do-Right* (1999), Canadian Mountie Dudley (Brendan Fraser) dreams that he is alone enjoying the beautiful countryside when he finds his beloved horse (which previously crashed through the wall of its stable because villain Snidely Whiplash [Alfred Molina] pretended to be a vampire). The Peaches & Herb song "Reunited" plays in the background of the dream as Dudley runs to his horse in slow motion with blurred color trailing behind his bright red Mountie jacket. Not only does Dudley find his best friend and partner again, but the horse tells him that there are no vampires in the woods, and that Whiplash has devised a gold rush scam in an effort to take over Semi-Happy Valley. The music provides more than a comical take on Dudley's dream, which is a wake-up call for the befuddled Mountie to "reunite" with his horse, his girlfriend, and his lost courage (overshadowed by Whiplash's false vampire scare). Part of the overall wish fulfillment dream, the song reveals his desperate need to overcome loneliness.

Creative Options

Superimpositions (one image over another, as in the blending of the two women's faces in *Persona* [1966]), slow motion (a reminder of REM paralysis, as in Claire's [Annette Bening's] lonely walk through a deserted town in *In Dreams*), dissolves (images that blend one scene into a similar scene through a matching or rippling effect, as in Catherine's [Jennifer Lopez's] dream in *The Cell* [2000] where lumps in her blanket dissolve into the sand dunes in a desert), and spiraling shapes and colors at the onset of a dream (*Altered States* [1980] and *Dreamscape* [1984]) represent just a few forms of distortion used to represent traditional dream sequences.

Because our eyes cannot zoom in and out like a camera, effects of this kind can produce highly dramatic results. "It is something like the effect that slow motion or stop motion has on us. It interrupts our perceptions of something — something that had seemed perfectly natural — in a way that makes us conscious of the film medium itself" (Martin and Jacobus, 403). Combining familiar effects, such as slow motion, black and white, fog, or garbled sound, makes us conscious of a dream sequence or altered state of mind. "We can't manipulate our eyes the way a camera can be adjusted to produce slow motion, fast motion, reverse motion, and freeze frames. Certainly our eyes have no real equivalents to dissolves, multiple exposures, negative images, distorting lenses and filters, focus manipulations, and all the other special effects that can be achieved through the use of the optical printer" (Giannetti, 1976, 437). In *Understanding Movies*, Giannetti defines the optical printer as an elaborate machine with a precisely aligned camera and projector that permit the operator to rephotograph all or part of an existing frame of a film.

In recent years, computer technology has surpassed the optical printer in providing creative options, greatly reducing the cost and increasing the abilities of filmmakers attempting to create surreal images in their films. Ben Rock, director and writer of the pseudo documentary telefilm *The Burkittsville 7* (2000), a tangential story to *The Blair Witch Project* (1999) for which he served as production designer, says post production has reached the point where directors can make decisions during the final stages of editing, rather than the early stages of shooting.

> The editing system has changed radically, specifically Avid [computer] editing allows you to change compositions, to change color schemes, to change almost anything while editing. You can make really hard decisions at the last stage of production where you can try different things. My editor on *The Burkittsville 7* was able to make a lot of the images we shot seem more weird, more surreal, more haunting by superimposing the same image five times and offsetting each one in one frame and making them all a little transparent ... or making all but one frame in black and white.[22]

Rock says programs such as Adobe After Effects allow filmmakers to add, stack, and effect elements, change focus or blur, and create a wide range of bizarre effects for dream sequences.

New computer technology enables directors to make important decisions alone in the comfort of an editing suite instead of under stress while the cast and crew impatiently wait and the cost increases by the minute. Although the director is the first to benefit from these technological advances, ultimately the audience profits as well. "These techniques keep the audience off balance because they don't know how to take it," Rock says. "The director gets a good solid image in the shoot and then messes with it in post to get exactly what he wants. You can bring in a piece of video and treat it in a million different ways that would have cost millions of dollars in opticals ten years ago."[23] This technology may help inspire filmmakers to replace dwarfs, smoke, and other overused elements in dream sequences— that actually bear no resemblance to actual dreams— with new visual and aural effects.

Chapter 15

Dream Symbols

In *Jurassic Park III* (2001), paleontologist Dr. Alan Grant (Sam Neill) has a dream while onboard a plane headed for doom, destruction, death, and dinosaurs, otherwise known as the tourist attraction Jurassic Park. In the dream, he wakes up to find a velociraptor talking to him. They are alone on the plane, and the cockpit is empty. He then wakes from the dream reassured to find a plane full of people, but immediately the trouble begins and we see that his dream was a warning, of sorts. An expert on dinosaur communication, his ability to "understand" velociraptors will eventually save his life.

The elements of this brief dream — a talking dinosaur, an empty plane, an awakening within a dream, and Grant's fear — combine visual and aural effects with Freud's five dreamwork processes to produce intriguing dream symbols. Freud's concept of displacement (redirecting thoughts, emotions, or urges from one person/object to another), condensation (merging people or places), symbolization (representing a repressed urge with a symbol), projection (moving our repressed desires onto other people), and secondary revision (constructing a story that connects the various elements during the final stage of the dream process) provide a blueprint for modern filmmakers in designing symbolic dream sequences.

Displacement

Displaced feelings lie at the core of *Vertigo*, and form the basis of the dreams experienced by Scottie Ferguson (James Stewart). A retired police detective, Scottie suffers from a debilitating fear of heights that forced him to resign from the police department. Soon afterwards, he is hired as a private detective to spy on the suicidal wife of Gavin Elster (Tom Helmore), a former school acquaintance. Elster's twenty-six-year-old wife, Madeleine

Poor confused Scottie (James Stewart) represses his feelings, then displaces them from Madeleine (the Kim Novak at left) to Carlotta to Judy (the Kim Novak at right) in *Vertigo* (Paramount Pictures Corporation, 1958).

(Kim Novak), seems possessed by the spirit of her great-grandmother, Carlotta Valdes, who committed suicide at the age of twenty-six. As Scottie follows her over the next few days, he falls deeply in love with Madeleine, yet is paralyzed with vertigo when she takes a suicidal jump from the top of a tower at an old Spanish mission. After her death, he is hospitalized for a mental breakdown.

During his convalescence, Scottie experiences a strange dream in which he watches a cartoon bouquet of roses rip into pieces, confuses the identity of Madeleine and Carlotta, visits the cemetery to see Madeleine's empty grave, and then sees his own disembodied head getting closer before his body falls onto a rooftop, then down into an endless spiral.

Months later, when he discovers Judy, the brash brunette woman who pretended to be the lovely platinum blonde Madeleine, Scottie insists that she wear the same clothes and fix her hair like Madeleine. He then falls deeply in love with her as well, until he learns that she was paid by Elster to play the part of Madeleine in order to facilitate killing his wife. *The Complete Hitchcock* (1999) describes Scottie as being only slightly less sinister than Elster. "It's not going too far to suggest that Scottie is a necrophiliac. Calling a dead lover back to life by giving another woman an erotic makeover is kinky at best, sick at worst" (Condon and Sangster, 1999, 223).

Perhaps Scottie is really just a hopeless romantic, inexperienced in matters of love and suffering from vertigo and post-traumatic stress. To help relieve his suffering, he represses his feelings and displaces them from Madeleine to Carlotta in his dream, then later from Madeleine to Judy. Realistically, Scottie loves neither Madeleine, Carlotta, nor Judy; he loves the woman whom Judy invented: a combination of the three.

In *Twelve Monkeys* (1995), a film in which the two fleeing characters take time out to watch *Vertigo* at the theater, time-traveling convict James Cole (Bruce Willis) has recurrent dreams of Dr. Kathryn Railly (Madeleine Stowe). James believes he is from the future and has dreamed of Kathryn all his life. He also dreams of airports, guns, and a spray-painted symbol of a monkey. As a psychiatrist, Kathryn says that he has displaced feelings towards the dream woman onto her so that now she has become the woman in his imagination. She is wrong, of course. As in *Vertigo*, no one knows the woman of his dreams better than the man who dreams her.

In *Twelve Monkeys*, a man (Bruce Willis) searching for the symbol of the Army of the Twelve Monkeys is ridiculed for confusing the woman of his dreams with a real woman (Universal City Studios, 1995). Photograph by Phil Caruso.

In the Tim Burton comedy *Pee-wee's Big Adventure* (1985), childlike Pee-wee Herman (Paul Reubens) is in love with his vintage red bicycle rather than a woman in his dreams. Each time he visits his favorite bicycle store and nearby magic shop, he carefully chains his prized possession to a life-sized mechanical clown in the parking lot. One day the bike mysteriously disappears, and he hallucinates that the clown laughs maniacally. During the next few days as he crosses the country in search of his bicycle, he has two nightmares. In the first dream, a claymation dinosaur devours his bike as distorted circus music plays in the background. He wakes shouting "No! No! Stop!"

Pee-wee's second dream, also accompanied by composer Danny Elfman's creepy circus music, begins with his broken bicycle lying on the wet ground. An ambulance arrives and three paramedics with clown faces and wigs arrive on the scene. With brightly colored neon lights illuminating the scene, they place the pieces on a stretcher, then wheel a gurney down a seemingly endless funhouse hallway. In the operating room, Pee-wee waits anxiously beneath a clock stuck at midnight as a doctor uses a blowtorch to operate on the broken bike. The doctor appears to give up hope, then lowers his mask to reveal his own painted clown face laughing hysterically at Pee-wee's predicament. The dream continues with Pee-wee's nemesis, Francis (Mark Holton), dressed as Satan, watching a crane lower the bike into a vat as demons dance and laugh amidst the fiery red heat and flames.

Discouraged by the police and his friends about recovering his stolen possession, and lied to by Francis (the actual culprit), Pee-wee represses his feelings of fear, grief, and anger. He takes these repressed feelings and unconsciously transfers them to the mechanical clown in the parking lot, and by association all clowns and events dealing with the circus. Although he suspects Francis of the crime, he cannot safely express his feelings towards the perpetrator. Hence, he symbolically envisions Francis as the devil, but displaces his most intense feelings onto the circus clowns in his dreams.

Condensation

Although condensation may involve the merging of any combination of people or places, filmmakers reveal a fondness for faces. In one of the dreams in *Wild Strawberries* (1957), the stuffed dummy Dr. Borg (Victor Sjostrom) encounters on the street has no face, yet the corpse in the coffin has the face of Dr. Borg. Similarly, his dreams and flashbacks to his first love, Sara, contain a beautiful young girl (Bibi Andersson) with the same face (and name) as the young hitchhiker whom he drives throughout the film. Dr. Borg's past, present, and future merge through repeated images of faces: his face, Sara's face, and a clock face with no hands.

In the Neil Jordan thriller *In Dreams*, Vivian Thompson (Robert Downey, Jr.) dreams of Claire (Annette Bening) while sleeping with her and his young kidnapping victim. His prophetic dream (see Chapter 10) shows an underwater point of view and then an aerial shot of a woman lying dead in a lake. When he wakes from the dream, he says, "My mommy was dead in the water, but she had your face." When Claire naively asks if that means he will kill her, he answers, "I hope not." In this dream, Vivian has repressed his violent urges towards his mother and Claire, condensing them into one chilling scene.

In *End of Days* (1999), Christine York (Robin Tunney) has a nightmare in which she has sex with the devil (Gabriel Byrne). The dream sequence begins with a clap of thunder as Satan writhes beneath the sheets with a mother and her daughter accompanied by loud rock music. The music changes as the scene turns into a dream, becoming increasingly threatening until it builds to a scary dream climax in which the woman's face underneath the devil becomes the face of Christine. This merging of identities—as exemplified through changing faces and melding bodies— condenses her sexual urges into the vilest image possible: sex with the devil. When the face becomes her own, the frightening image breaks through the sleep guardian and wakes Christine from her nightmare.

Bryne says the scene transforms from his character's reality into Christine's nightmare, both figuratively and literally. "The perspective of the character determines how dreams or visions are set apart from the rest of the film. Usually dreams and visions are outside the narrative reality of the film and they will use a technique to indicate that the film has now gone into dream, daydream, or vision."[24] In the case of Christine's nightmare, the visual effects include strange computer-enhanced morphing of the writhing, naked bodies and the aural effects include thunder and frightening music that changes within the dream sequence. These elements— combined with the surprising shift to her face — set the scene apart from the narrative reality of a lonely young woman with no one to trust and allow Christine a safe place to engage in her perverse fantasy.

Merging and shifting faces also plays an important part in the intricate story line of *Vanilla Sky* (2001). The face of publisher David Aames (Tom Cruise) shifts back and forth from handsome to disfigured; we (and David) never know what he will find when he looks into the mirror. Similarly, the face of his love interest (Penelope Cruz) changes at the most inconvenient times to that of his ex-girlfriend (Cameron Diaz), a scorned woman driven to madness by David's casual affair with her. The identities of the two women and the two identities of David are condensed in the dreams he does not know he is dreaming.

Symbolization

In *Jump Tomorrow* (2000), George (Tunde Adebimpe) is an introverted, inarticulate African-American man days away from his arranged marriage to a childhood friend when he meets Alicia (Natalia Verbeke), an exciting Spanish girl who invites him to a party and changes his life. Throughout the storybook love that the film depicts, fantasy and dream sequences reveal the repressed George beneath the shy exterior: He longs to be a strong, virile hero of a telenovella, shouting commands in Spanish. According to Joel Hopkins, the writer and director of *Jump Tomorrow* and *Jorge* (1998), the short film on which the feature is based, these sequences were shot on Beta, then played on television, then filmed from the television screen to give them a grainy, dreamlike quality with a bluish background to symbolize how George feels about himself.

"The fantasy and dream sequences were crucial for the character of George, this introverted quiet man, because we have very little access to what he's really thinking," Hopkins says. "Through these fantasies we can see inside his head. It's another way to get into the character without resorting to voice-over narration. People in audiences have told me 'That was our way into George. We really got behind him once we saw his fantasies.'"[25] Because George falls in love with a Spanish girl, Hopkins decided that telenovellas would express the character's fascination with the woman and her culture, which reflect the opposite of his current life.

According to Adebimpe, other than speaking fluent Spanish in the fantasy and dream sequences, shooting the scenes was much like shooting other scenes in the film. The look of the fantasy and dream sequences was established through camera techniques and skillful editing, in addition to the acting. "I was supposed to be daydreaming, then dead asleep, then in some kind of altered state," Adebimpe says. "The audience sees the sleeping George, then cuts to the fantasy George. The grainy television look and the Spanish let you know right away that something strange is going on."[26]

Besides a distinctive look, the sequences are introduced with their own distinctive sound. Hopkins says, "I found a jet engine sound that I used in conjunction with a snap zoom in these sequences. We accompany these with the jet engine 'whoosh' kind of sound to establish the sequences."[27]

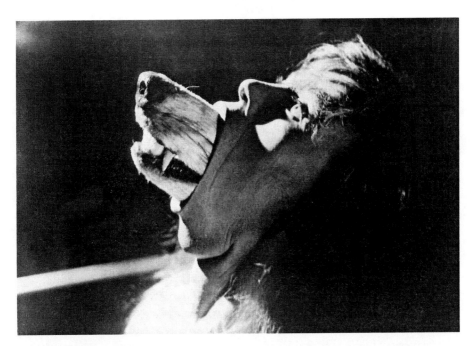

One of the most popular symbols in dream sequences, an animal represents a manifestation of inner urges in a young girl's dream in *The Company of Wolves* (ITC Entertainment, 1984).

The powerful jet engine combined with the heroic dream character symbolize what George is capable of becoming with the love of Alicia.

Popular dream symbols in film: Mirrors reflect a repressed self-image (*Wild Strawberries, Persona* [1966]; *Cries and Whispers* [1972]; *Picnic at Hanging Rock* [1975], *The Sender* [1982], *The Company of Wolves* [1984], *In Dreams, Shattered Image* [1998], *Warlock 3* [1998], *Stir of Echoes* [1999], *The Cell* [2000], *Vanilla Sky*); animals represent inner urges (*Altered States* [1980], *Cat People* [1982], *The Company of Wolves, Another Woman* [1988], *Snow Dogs* [2002]); apples reveal innocence corrupted (*The Company of Wolves, Living in Oblivion* [1994], *In Dreams, End of Days*); clocks mean time passage (*Wild Strawberries, Cries and Whispers, Picnic at Hanging Rock, Pee-wee's Big Adventure, Living in Oblivion, The Cell, Lara Croft: Tomb Raider* [2001]); and windows, doors, and stairs offer past and future escape (*Marnie* [1964], *Persona* [1966], *Despair* [1977], *Risky Business* [1983], *A Nightmare on Elm Street* [1984], *Dreamscape* [1984], *Living in Oblivion, The Cell*).

One of the most important symbols used in dream sequences, however, is color. Ever since Dorothy (Judy Garland) first tapped her ruby red slippers together in her colorful dream in *The Wizard of Oz* (1939), filmmakers have added color, deleted color, or used monochromatic dream sequences to set them apart from the rest of the film. Sleep expert Dement writes:

> Some aspects of what people think about dreaming are the result of imperfect recall. A good example of this is the fact that many people believe we dream in black and white, like an old movie. However, years ago I was able to show that people dreamed in color and could remember the color if they reported dreams immediately upon being awakened from REM periods. Apparently the memory for color faded faster than everything else [1999, 297].

Sleep scientists agree that sighted people dream in color, despite protestations to the contrary.

Even so, manipulating the color in filmed dream sequences makes a powerful symbolic statement regarding the dreamer's state of the mind. "The sayings, 'seeing red,' 'feeling blue,' 'green with envy,' and black with rage,' all relate to actual changes which take place in the colours of our own electro-magnetic field due to changes in our emotions," according to Mary Anderson in *Colour Therapy* (1990, 15). Applying commonly believed logic of color therapy to red, the most prominent filmic dream color, shades of red symbolize excitement, activity, stimulation, desire, and violence associated with the heart, blood, and blood pressure.

Cries and Whispers, Ingmar Bergman's enigmatic film about a dying young woman, her servant, and her two repressed sisters, effectively blends dreams, fantasies, flashbacks, and reality about the four unhappy women who temporarily must share time and space with each other. The house in which nearly every scene occurs— both real and imagined — has red tablecloths, chairs, drapes, and walls. Each dream sequence begins and ends with a flash of red, and many include a chiming clock and soft female whispers. In a film concerned with deception, loneliness, illusions, and death, these visual and aural cues respectively symbolize our hidden passions, the passage of time, and the secrets we all hide. Bergman has said he imagined the soul as "a moist red membrane" and shades of red dominate nearly every scene in the film (Eastman, 1989, 71). Even the opening credits appear over a red background.

The color red also plays a prominent part in the background of troubling dreams in *Vertigo*, *Cat People*, *Pee-wee's Big Adventure*, and *Total Recall* (1990). Selective use of red symbols within dreams include the red capes (of innocent young women) in *The Company of Wolves* and *In Dreams*, both directed by Neil Jordan. *In Dreams* also includes dreams of hundreds of red apples, red high heels, and the death of a girl named Ruby. Flashes of red in the dreams in *Marnie* symbolize the blood of a repressed murder.

In keeping with this line of reasoning, how can we explain Freddy Krueger's ever-present red and green striped sweater throughout the *Nightmare* series? When discussing the seven major cosmic rays, Anderson writes that the red ray "supplies our physical bodies with energy and vitality. It is drawn through the base chakra [power center] at the root of the spine," i.e., genitals. She describes green as "the colour of nature, of balance, peace and harmony…. This is the ray which is absorbed by the *heart chakra* and controls the *cardiac centre*. Green is a mixture of blue and yellow, and strongly influences the heart and blood pressure" (Anderson, 1990, 39–42). Therefore, Freud might say that the red and green represent Krueger's (and our) two basic instincts— repressed while awake and symbolized while asleep — sexual and aggressive urges.

The color blue usually symbolizes cool, restful, calming scenes that actually lower our pulse and respiration — sometimes to the point of death. *In Dreams* uses red apples and red capes for dreams of current violence. However, when Claire (Annette Bening) dreams of Vivian Thompson's past, she envisions an underwater tomb devoid of color except the restful blue of the water from the dam that flooded his home. Later as Claire drowns, she looks through the blue-tinted water to see her dead daughter telling her to come home to heaven.

Christian J. Otjen, writer and director of *Frightened to Death* (1987) and *Lady in the Box* (2000) says dreams are an effective way of getting the audience into the mind of the characters. "In *Frightened to Death*, the character has a scary dream in order to get one message across: He feels fear. I added a blue tint to the dream sequence during post production to make it have a dreamlike quality. I didn't want to give it away — only just a hint that maybe it wasn't real." Otjen says using dream sequences of any color should be a deliberate attempt to solve a particular cinematic problem, rather than a ready-made solution. "Usually the message could be delivered through better writing than through dream sequences."[28]

In *Sleepy Hollow* (1999), the dark, dreary, colorless environment of Sleepy Hollow reflects the cloud of doom and death that hangs over the area since the Headless Horseman arrived to seek revenge on the townspeople. When Ichabod Crane (Johnny Depp) comes to investigate the decapitation murders, he briefly escapes the daily misery with his colorful dreams of the past. Bathed in warm sunlight and saturated with rich colors, he dreams of his bewitched mother and the love they shared before she was murdered during a witch hunt.

Living in Oblivion portrays the making of a low-budget independent film in a three-part story. The first part is the director's dream, a nightmare about chaos on the set that is shot in black and white. Within his dream, the scenes being filmed are in color. The second part of the movie represents the star's dream, an embarrassing one-night stand with her costar that is shot in color. Within her dream, the scenes being filmed are in black and white. The third part of the movie, shot entirely in color, is reality, i.e., the cast is assembled to shoot a dream sequence. In director Tom DiCillo's amusing and confusing look behind the scenes of independent filmmaking, color helps disguise reality and illusion.

Projection

In Ingmar Bergman's *Cries and Whispers*, four women in confined quarters cannot openly express their feelings, instead relying on dreams, daydreams, and flashbacks to escape their present realities and transfer their repressed feelings. One woman is a servant and the other three are wealthy sisters—one sexually repressed, one promiscuous, and one dying from disease. Anna (Kari Sylwan) the lowly servant whose child recently died, dreams that the dying sister, Agnes (Harriet Andersson), for whom she works, needs her help during the transition from life to death. Agnes' two sisters, Karin (Ingrid Thulin) and Maria (Liv Ullmann), prove unable to cope with the reality of death, while Anna provides the loving comfort of a mother to a child — her lost child perhaps— for the ailing woman. Anna lovingly cradles Agnes against her naked breast in what appears to be her dream.

Within the dream, which may be shared by one or all of the women, the dead Agnes calls for help as her soul leaves her body. She assures her servant that while it may be only a dream for Anna, it is real for Agnes. "The dream sequence in *Cries and Whispers* creates the impression of being a composite dream: a dream of each of the characters as well as the filmmaker. For Anna it is a dream of wish-fulfillment; for Karin and Maria, a dream of (unpleasant) self-revelation" (Maxfield, 1998, 65). Interpreting the dream as a single wish fulfillment for Anna, the scene exhibits her projected feelings onto her dying patient. Despite lifelong bonds to her sisters, Agnes can find comfort, love, and peace in the arms of Anna alone.

In another Bergman film, *Persona*, a young nurse, Alma (Bibi Andersson), obsessively dreams and hallucinates that she and her silent psychiatric patient Elisabeth (Liv Ullmann) share loves, laughs, secrets, intimate embraces, the same husband, and even the same face.

As the women draw closer, Bergman photographs them in complementary costumes, uses parallel set-ups, and even blocks their movement so that their bodies seem to merge. This "doubles" motif is carried over into a dream sequence (probably Alma's) in which Elisabeth enters the nurse's room through one door and leaves through another parallel to it. Photographed mostly in slow motion through a gauzy lens, this graceful sequence is one of the first overt dramatizations of the merging of personalities. Both women stand before a dark mirror, where Elisabeth pulls back Alma's hair to reveal their extraordinary physical resemblance [Giannetti, 1976, 363].

Sadly, Elisabeth is merely amused by her nurse's devotion. When Alma reads an unkind letter Elisabeth writes about her, she painfully realizes that their relationship is merely a projection of her repressed desires, rather than a mutual admiration, and seeks revenge through a mixture of dreams, hallucinations, and reality.

The sadomasochistic dreams and daydreams of Parisian newlywed Severine (Catherine Deneuve) in *Belle de Jour* (1967) also represent projection of repressed feelings onto others. Although subdued Severine loves her handsome doctor husband, she cannot feel passion with his polite advances and respectful demeanor. In her dreams, he is a brutal tyrant who insults her, then orders his servants to whip her, rape her, and throw mud in her face. Although we see no indication that her husband would ever resort to such behavior in reality, her dream husband is a projection of her hidden need for degradation.

Secondary Revision

Although Freud says secondary revision takes place during the final stages of dream production shortly before awakening, cinematic dreams combine the logical and illogical after awakening, as the character explains the dream to someone else. Because these dreams usually abide by the dramatic story structure outlined by Jung (as discussed in Chapter 3), which progresses from exposition, development, and culmination to the solution or result, they are either shown in narrative story form in real time or described that way in retrospect by the dreamer.

Without the visual effects, however, retelling a dream sequence (real or feigned) has more impact on the characters than it does on the audience. *Fiddler on the Roof* (1971) overcomes this problem by recreating the dream that Tevye (Chaim Topol) says he experienced. Although we know the dream is manufactured for the sake of his wife, we can enjoy its dramatic elements. Fake dreams also play a part in *Vertigo*, where ironically,

Madeleine (Kim Novak) tells Scottie (James Stewart) about frightening dreams that she does not really experience, and Scottie does not tell Madeleine about seemingly recurrent frightening dreams that he does experience.

In the beginning scenes of the noir-style thriller *Lady in the Box*, a young bartender named Jerry Halway (Darren E. Burrows) growls into his girlfriend's ear while she sleeps in order to induce nightmares which will make her cling to him for comfort. When Jill (Paige Rowland) awakens minutes later, she tells Jerry in a slow seductive voice as she unbuttons her blouse:

> I was having a bad dream. Bogeyman stuff. But now you're here so it's ok... Someone was watching me in my dream. Someone outside... It was like he was here in this room. He was undressing me. I can almost smell him. Do you know that feeling? Like when you know you're going to do something bad. And you think about it and you get nervous and you're wondering what if somebody's watching. What if someone sees? What if you get caught? You feel your palms getting sweaty and you have goose bumps on your skin. Your hair stands on end. You're waiting ... waiting ... What if someone was watching, Jerry? What would you do?

In keeping with the noir tradition of femme fatales and sappy men who fall into their traps, Jerry ignores the inherent warning in her dream (or at least in her recounting the supposed nightmare to him) and seems intrigued and maybe a little guilty for growling in her ear.

As the disturbing story unfolds and Jill becomes Jerry's figurative nightmare, we doubt that Jill's dream actually occurred. Christian J. Otjen, who wrote and directed the film, says, "The dream was a fake to toy with Jerry, and to set him up for the following night. I tried to write her dialogue so it paralleled the thoughts of Jerry, i.e., doing something wrong, what if someone were watching, as well as what might have been a real dream."[29] Her secondary revision — actually a complete concoction — confuses Jerry and the audience, while Jill maintains complete control.

Similarly, Diana (Uma Thurman) fakes recurring dreams in *Final Analysis* in order to gain the sympathy of Dr. Barr (Richard Gere). The opening lines of the film are spoken by Diana as she lies on the psychiatrist's couch for an extreme close-up as she describes her dream to Dr. Barr. Accompanied by soft background music, she says: "I had the dream again. I'm arranging flowers on a table for a centerpiece. I decorate the flower pot with fancy paper. It feels like velvet. There are three different kinds of flowers. There are lilies, and there are ... by the way, did you reach my sister...." The music abruptly stops, traffic noises intrude, and the

A young bartender (Darren E. Burrows) tries to give his girlfriend nightmares, but she cleverly reverses the situation in *Lady in the Box* (Doomed Productions, 2000). Courtesy of Christian J. Otjen.

camera zooms back to include the entire scene. The dream ends and reality takes over.

In a later scene, Diana reports the same dream that she claims is her own, though it actually comes from the pages of Freud's *The Interpretation of Dreams*. This time she reveals lilies, carnations, and violets in the arrangement, and says, "the dream ends with everything going up in flames — one big fireball." Again soft music and diffused light accompany her dream, which is described, not shown. Although Dr. Barr obviously feels great compassion for his patient, we can sense that something is wrong from the opening lines of the film, because the dream is described rather than shown.

Rich with symbols and enhanced by lighting and sound effects, Diana's dream still does not ring true. If her dream is so important, then why is it reduced to a mere description? The answer comes far later in the film when we (and eventually Dr. Barr) realize the dream is not real. To really touch the audience, we must see and hear the dream sequence — even retrospectively as in *Spellbound* (1945) — in order to gauge its emotional truth.

The opening dream sequence in *Risky Business* (1983), told retrospectively and shown in glorious detail, reveals the truth about the teenaged character's anguished emotional state. Tom Cruise (as Joel Goodsen) begins: "The dream is always the same...." He then describes the recurring dream in which he enters a neighbor's house and finds a beautiful girl taking a shower in the upstairs bathroom. She invites him to wash her back, but as he walks toward her, the steam from the shower blinds him. When he finally arrives at the door, the shower is empty, and the scene shifts to a classroom where students are taking college board exams. He realizes he missed the entire test because of his preoccupation with sexual desires. Accompanied by the surreal music of Tangerine Dream, the dream sequence reveals the emotional truth concerning the entire film: Joel's anxiety about the future, desire for sexual wish fulfillment, and conflicted emotions.

Dream elements have been included in dream sequences since they first appeared in early films around 1900. Advances in modern technology permit easier depiction of these elements, but in keeping with Jungian theory, the same universal dream symbols appear year after year in every style of film from every country. Although many directors explore dreams on film, because of his devotion to Freudian theories of dreamwork and symbolic use of image, color, and sound in dreams, Alfred Hitchcock is still considered by many to be the master of the dream sequence.

While thrillers such as *Final Analysis* (1992), *Twelve Monkeys* (1995), and *With a Friend Like Harry* (2000) openly pay tribute to Hitchcock films, these recent movies had an advantage. "The director can reveal the unconscious fears and desires of his characters through good writing or visually, like through a Dalí dream sequence as Hitchcock did," according to Henry Bromell, writer and director of *Panic* (2000). "Hitchcock created psychological states of mind by the way he shot scenes— all scenes, including his dream sequences. New computers make creating strange dreams much easier. Hitchcock had to work much harder to make a dream sequence than we do now."[30] Whether these dream elements are produced with old-fashioned camera tricks or the latest computer technology, cinematic dreams still rely on Freudian dreamwork processes.

Chapter 16

Reality vs. Illusion

Directors create reality and illusion within each film; we interpret what is real and what is dreamed by interpreting filmic cues and applying our own memories, perceptions, points of view, and self-awareness. In *Marnie* (1964), a beautiful young frigid bride (Tippi Hedren) has recurrent nightmares about vile sailors banging on the window for her prostitute mother. With the love, patience, and armchair psychoanalytic dream interpretation of her husband, Mark Rutland (Sean Connery), she eventually is able to overcome her frigidity, and a host of other ills such as kleptomania, pathological lying, fear of thunderstorms, and an aversion to the color red. Throughout the film, Marnie confuses past and present, reality and illusion, and dreams and wakefulness, although we easily can tell the difference. Her dreams occur when she sleeps; her phobias and hallucinations appear irrational to us and to the other characters in the movie.

In Spanish director Luis Buñuel's French film *Belle de Jour* (1972), however, Severine (Catherine Deneuve) apparently knows the difference between her dreams and reality, but we do not. A wealthy chic wife of a handsome young doctor, she is a frigid newlywed, aroused only by her recurring dreams and daydreams of prostitution, sexual abuse, and personal degradation. Some of her dreams are clearly identified as such — Severine is shown sleeping and waking up. Ringing bells precede these recurring dream sequences of a horse-drawn carriage in which she, her husband, and the coachmen ride. The carriage, costumes, and open countryside seem long ago and far away — a sexual fantasy land where she can safely indulge in the behavior she craves.

Yet other scenes defy classification as dreams, daydreams, or reality. When Severine begins filling her lonely afternoons as a prostitute at a high-class brothel, many REM state characteristics apply, in accordance with the IUD (incongruity, uncertainty, and discontinuity) scale. Incongruities include the beautiful, delicate Severine actually taking pleasure in sex with the metal-toothed thug who fancies her; uncertainties include why her husband finds a wheelchair on the street so fascinating (a wheelchair that he will eventually be confined to); and discontinuities include Severine's sleeping, daydreaming, and waking states which are indistinct and indiscriminate.

In *Belle de Jour*, the mismatches in logic, unknown dream elements, and abnormal shifts in action make it impossible to distinguish waking from dreaming, reality from illusion. Therefore, the end of the film, which provides two completely different options, remains indecipherable. Does the thug shoot her husband, leaving him catatonic in a wheelchair or does her husband playfully jump up from the wheelchair which formed the basis for her daydreams about the metal-toothed thug?

The question of reality is addressed in Leo Braudy's book *The World in a Frame* (1977): "Too often we accept a film as a window on reality without noticing that the window has been opened in a particular way, to exclude as well as to include" (22). This window on reality may include or exclude dream elements that confuse the audience about the reality of the situation. We know when Marnie is dreaming because her reality makes logical sense and contains no dream elements. For Severine, dream elements such as ringing bells, a high-class brothel, misogynistic patrons, and a deserted wheelchair on a city street present strange — though believable — elements of reality or dreams. Her dreams in the country are obviously dreams, but the rest of the film is shrouded in doubt.

In his essay "Double Lives," Michael Wood mentions an introductory note to the script of *Belle de Jour* which says the dreamlike sequences will not be distinguished from other surrounding sequences by either image or sound.

> This isn't quite how the film plays, since several of Severine's fantasies have a period flavor — the coach, an old-fashioned necrophiliac duke, a duel in frockcoats — while others have clear internal markings of the imaginary: whippings which don't score the back, speech coming from a closed mouth [1992, 22].

Although Severine likely recognizes reality and illusion, for us her dreams have no clear beginning, middle, or ending.

A film's visual and aural effects (as discussed in Chapter 14) usually alert the audience that the character is entering a dream state and the following scene should not be interpreted as literal truth. When we see a close-up of someone's face tossing and turning on a pillow then a kaleidoscope of spiraling or shifting colors we anticipate a dream sequence. When a bizarre story with incongruity, uncertainty, and discontinuity surrounding some sort of wish fulfillment follows, and then ends abruptly at the height of action, we know without a doubt that the character is dreaming. An additional effect, the sleeping intercut as used in *The Company of Wolves* (1984) and *Lara Croft: Tomb Raider* (2001) among countless others, also helps remind us that the character is indeed dreaming and the images should be evaluated symbolically and emotionally, rather than literally and intellectually.

When directors purposely leave out these cues until the end of the dream sequence, however, we momentarily confuse reality and illusion, like the characters in the scene. Films such as *The Princess Bride* (1987), *Living in Oblivion* (1994), *Analyze This* (1998), and *Stir of Echoes* (1999) catch us off guard by cuing us after a dream instead of before. In the 1982 Paul Schrader-directed thriller *Cat People*, Irena (Nastassja Kinski) drifts off to sleep on a train and has a vivid dream. We see a fiery red, barren landscape with black panthers lounging in the trees—the land of her unusual heritage of incest and bestiality, and her apparent destiny, as well. Breaking the usual tradition of surprising the audience with an abrupt awakening, Schrader surprises us by showing her falling asleep but never awakening, which leaves us to wonder how much of the ending is a dream and how much is real.

When directors purposely exclude these cues throughout the entire film, we are left in a hazy, muddled state of our own, left to interpret, decipher, and analyze without the benefit of dreamers awakening with a shout and explaining to someone what their dream meant. Films including *8½* (1963), *Belle de Jour*, *Persona* (1966), *Cries and Whispers* (1972), *Picnic at Hanging Rock* (1975), *Despair* (1977), *The Sender* (1982), *The Company of Wolves* (1984), *Shattered Image* (1998), and *Vanilla Sky* (2001) continually move back and forth through time, space, and consciousness without definitive cues.

For the careful observer, science and art work together in dream sequences, determining reality and illusion — or at least helping explain the reasons for confusion. A few of the many factors involved in this complicated process of deciphering filmic waking and dreaming include memory, perception, point of view, and self-awareness (lucidity).

Dreams as Memory

Like our memories of cinematic images, our memories of dreams change over time. Robert T. Eberwein writes in his book, *Film and the Dream Screen: A Sleep and a Forgetting*, (1984): "The longer we are away from the film, the more confused our memories of it become. In fact, the difficulty that presents itself as we try to recall the events and details of a film seems similar to that which we encounter as we try to remember dreams" (5). This lack of total recall combines with perception, point of view, and self-awareness to distort dreamed images, sometimes to the point of blurring reality and illusion. "Since dreams are (among other things) memories, in retrospect it is often impossible to distinguish with absolute certainty if a memory reflects a real event or a dream" (Dee, 1990, 37).

When film characters wander through scene after scene terrorized by their dreams and visions, or are unsure whether they are awake or dreaming, we can appreciate their predicament because we have been there ourselves— almost. "The absence of self-consciousness found in both sleepwalking and night terrors might be related to the global amnesia that people sometimes experience with extreme sleep deprivation. After all, perception is so intimately tied to memory that it is difficult to separate them" (Dement and Vaughan, 1999, 212). Watching films in a naturally produced altered state of consciousness allows viewers to make creative connections and experience emotional resonance with characters. Our vague feelings of remembered empathy mix with current feelings of sympathy while watching their struggles to determine what is real.

In *The Sender* (1982), a young male amnesiac telepathically sends his nightmares to others while they are awake. The audience and the film characters who receive these horrifying nightmares are unable to tell reality from illusion. When a doctor at the state mental hospital where John Doe (Zeljko Ivanek) is staying drills a hole into his head for some experimental surgery, the operating room simultaneously bursts into flames and the doctor is swept off his feet by the unseen power of the young man's dream. Although logic tells us otherwise, the nurses, attendants, doctors, and especially the surgeon hanging from the ceiling believe John Doe's telepathic dreams are real. The final scene in the film, where the young man rides off in a truck with his dead mother, whom apparently is alive and well to him, suggests that he also cannot separate his dreams from reality. Perhaps director Roger Christian purposely blurs dream and reality in order to keep us interested in his low-tech horror flick until its chilling ending, or maybe our confusion reflects the disturbed mental state of a young patient whose memory of fact and fiction has been erased.

While *The Sender* examines a young telepathic amnesiac who has forgotten what is real, *Wild Strawberries* (1957) introduces us to an old man who finally faces reality by remembering his past. Dr. Isak Borg (Victor Sjostrom) acts as narrator of his story, telling us: "I may even have begun to remember my childhood. How it happened, I don't know, but the clear reality of day gave way to the still clearer images of memory which arose before my eyes with all the force of reality." These images take the form of fantasies while he is awake and dreams while he is asleep. Although the memories arise with the force of reality, Dr. Borg never confuses reality and illusion. In keeping with Freudian theory of dreams as repressed wishes, these memories—a mixture of painful and pleasurable—come to the cold, isolated, egoist in the only form he will receive them: altered states of consciousness over which he has no control.

Perception of Reality

The dreaming mind and parts of the dreaming body perceive dreams as reality. Unless we are experiencing lucid dreaming in which self-awareness allows us to manipulate dream elements to our advantage, our mind convinces our emotions that what we experience in our dreams is real (while we are dreaming). Studies in sleep laboratories also have shown that the unparalyzed eyes during REM sleep receive orders from the brain to react to dream scenes the same way they would to reality.

During REM sleep beneath closed lids without any external stimuli, eyes will move back and forth to watch imagined tennis matches, raise to peer into a dreamed sky, or react appropriately to any perceived scene. "To certain parts of the brain, there is no difference between waking life and dreaming life. When we are dreaming of eating or fighting or thinking, the brain is sending out the same signals it would if we were awake and eating or fighting or thinking" (Dement and Vaughan, 1999, 299). Our inability to remember most dreams and our ability to perceive that what we dreamed was unreal, permit most of us to clearly distinguish what is real and what is imagined.

This link between memory and perception works well cinematically. According to writer-director Ben Rock, blending the two in flashbacks, dreams, and daydreams makes these scenes more expressive.

> In *The Burkittsville 7*, I tried to show scenes the way someone would actually remember it, not literally as if it were a real event. If I'm having a flashback to a conversation that I had, I won't remember all the details but I will remember things happening a certain way.... I like to see flashbacks that also take on a much more subjective position than flashbacks that show what would have happened if there had been a documentary camera. Modern viewers understand that a movie is from someone's point of view. I like to see flashbacks that are clearly subjective from one person's point of view and contrast that perception with the rest of the film.[31]

Incorporating the characters' perceptions into flashbacks, dreams, and day-dreams makes them more visually exciting and meaningful for the audience, Rock says. "My biggest problems with dream sequences is that they generally are too literal. They don't show things in a dream language, they show them in regular movie language with dolly shots and good lighting."[32] Using dream language during dream sequences also helps the audience and the dreamer separate the dream from reality.

Even when film characters can separate their dreams from reality, they are punished by society for believing that some elements in the dream can reflect reality. Hospitalized for her recurrent nightmares about a serial killer, Claire Cooper (Annette Bening) in *In Dreams* (1998) must convince her husband, psychiatrist, and a team of doctors that she is not crazy — that her clairvoyant dreams reflect the future reality. She tells her doctor: "He's feeding me dreams. I'm not obsessed; I'm possessed." Although driven to a suicide attempt by her dreams and hallucinations, essentially her perceptions are correct: Her dreams are reality being telepathically transmitted by a psychopath played by Robert Downey, Jr. He confirms all her doubts, and answers all her questions with one line spoken shortly after they meet face to face for the first time: "I've been looking for another dreamer out there like me."

In *Terminator 2: Judgment Day* (1991), Sarah Conner (Linda Hamilton) endures years of incarceration in maximum security at Pescadero State Mental Hospital because she claims to know the future. She says self-aware robots will destroy most of humanity with a nuclear holocaust so they can control the world with deadly Terminators, designed for one purpose: to destroy every living human. Sarah knows the truth because she has been visited in the previous film *The Terminator* (1984) by a man and killer robot from the future. With the man dead and the robot incinerated, she now suffers from nightmares of the past (and future), but her psychiatrist tries to convince her that her dreams have no basis in reality.

In a videotaped interview with her doctor, Sarah, wrapped in a straitjacket, responds to her doctor's disbelief and condescension. "The dream's the same every night, why do I have to..."

"Please continue...," says Dr. Silberman.

"The children look like burnt paper ... black, not moving. Then the blast wave hits them and they fly apart like leaves...," Sarah cries.

"Dreams about cataclysm, or the end of the world are very common, Sarah —"

She cuts him off, her mood shifting to sudden rage. "It's not just a dream when it's real. I know the date it happens!"

"I'm sure it feels very real to you —"

Sarah screams: "On August 29th 1997 it's gonna feel pretty fucking real to you, too! Anybody not wearing two million sunblock is gonna have a real bad day—get it? God! You think you're alive and safe, but you're already dead. Everybody... Him... You... You're dead already!... You're the one living in the fucking dream, Silberman."

Whose perception of reality would not be distorted by doctors telling them that reality was an illusion? In Sarah's case, her doctor goes one step further and tells her that reality and dreams (that reflect that reality) are illusions. Eventually Sarah's bulging biceps, keen intellect, strong will, and belief in her own perceptions overpower the doctor, and she breaks out of the hospital in order to prepare for the future revealed in her nightmares.

Point of View

The point of view from which we witness a dream differs from our perception, which explores how the mind convinces our emotions that something is real. A first-person point of view makes a highly convincing element in dreams because it is scientifically accurate and, therefore, contains psychological truth; the only problem is that most filmed dream sequences do not view the dream through the eyes of the dreamer.

When innocent young newlywed Rosemary (Mia Farrow) in Roman Polanski's *Rosemary's Baby* (1968) has a drug-induced nightmare that a hideous hairy beast rapes her as people chant and cheer on the sidelines, we see some of the action from an omniscient point of view and some from a first-person perspective, i.e., the camera reveals an objective viewpoint of the entire scene from a distance and a subjective viewpoint from the eyes of the terrified rape victim. At one point in the dream, she cries out desperately: "This is no dream! This is really happening!" Although the scene does feel real, because of its varied points of view and dream elements, we and Rosemary are never really sure if the scene is real or imagined until the end of the film.

Writer-director Ben Rock cites this dream sequence from *Rosemary's Baby* as a good example of effectively using point of view. "Dream sequences should feel dreamlike because they represent the weird meandering thoughts that coalesce into visuals in the mind. You see this subjective scene from Rosemary's point of view when they pull her pants off and you can feel her terror."[33] Effective or not, lengthy scenes from the first-person point of view are rare in dream sequences.

Virtually all filmed dream sequences depict most—if not all—scenes from an omniscient point of view. Showing the entire scene objectively and omnisciently (at least at first) establishes the scene, the characters, and the dreamer for the audience, and more importantly, allows the star additional screen time. In actual dreams, we hardly ever see ourselves and almost never dream that we are someone else, an animal, or an inanimate object. Although the dream world is surreal, we are not. "In normal dreams, particularly those of young children, the dreamer does not usually appear in the dream. It is very important to note that lucid dreams can emerge out of any dream, and that emergence is self-reflection" (The Dalai Lama, 1997, 101). As discussed above in the section on perception of reality, our unparalyzed eyes perceive the tennis match itself, not a vision of ourselves watching the tennis match.

Although scientific accuracy and psychological truth call for first-person dream sequences, additional reasons exist for presenting different points of view. In *The Princess Bride* (1987), the omniscient point of view tricks us into thinking that Buttercup (Robin Wright) actually marries the "warthog-faced buffoon" who plans to kill her and start a war. Had we seen visual/aural cues or watched the scene through her horrified eyes, we would have realized the scene was a dream and might not have shared the momentary sense of anger, disappointment, and betrayal that she had already married the vile prince.

Similarly, the omniscient point of view and blend of hallucinations, nightmares, and visions keep us guessing in *Warlock 3: The End of Innocence* (1998). After inheriting an old house and moving in for a few days, Kris Miller (Ashley Laurence) sees ghostly images of a little girl and her doll, distorted images of herself in a mirror, and gruesome scenes of her slaughtered friends in visions and nightmares. Reality and illusion are so confused in this film that we cannot discern what is real and what is dreamed, or to whom these dreams belong. If we saw everything from Kris's point of view, much of the mystery would be solved.

We can feel much safer in *A Nightmare on Elm Street* (1984) because Nancy (Heather Langenkamp) appears in her own dreams. If we saw the disfigured, razor-clawed demon chasing us only from a first-person perspective, the fear might be overwhelming. This way, we can relax a little because part of us knows that Freddy Krueger (Robert Englund) is chasing her, not us.

In *The Talented Mr. Ripley* (1999), Tom Ripley (Matt Damon) has nightmares that are neither shown nor described. We are aware of his nightmares, however, because the camera pans wildly around the room as he sleeps fitfully on the couch. His repressed guilt, expressed through his unconscious dream state, tells of his instability and assures us that he suffers (at least inwardly) for his crimes.

Lucid Dreaming

According to *The Promise of Sleep*, one in five people have lucid (self-aware) dreams naturally during REM sleep, although they tend to be short-lived experiences occurring just before awakening. A condition that was first studied in detail in the 1970s by Stephen LaBerge, director of the Lucidity Institute in Palo Alto, California, lucid dreaming is knowing that we are dreaming as we dream, which enables us to exhibit some control over the content of the dream. "Lucid dreamers report that they can make themselves fly through walls and over houses, that they are able to practice the piano, take vacations to specific locales, and arrange sexual encounters, all while deep in REM sleep" (Dement and Vaughan, 1999, 323). With training and practice, approximately sixty percent of the population can develop lucid dreaming skills.

In *The Lucid Dreamer* (1994), Malcolm Godwin writes, "The actual imagery experienced in this state is often claimed to be far more vivid and full of life than in normal, non-lucid states and it is extremely difficult for even the most veteran lucid dreamers to ascertain whether the experience is a waking reality or not" (10). Lucid dreamers on film are always at risk of losing themselves in the dream indefinitely or dying — whichever comes first.

When film characters go to the trouble of becoming self-aware in their dreams, it is usually a matter of life and death. *Dreamscape* (1984), *The Cell* (2000), and all of the *A Nightmare on Elm Street* movies feature lucid dreamers fighting for their lives. In *Dreamscape*, dream-linking psychic Alex Gardner (Dennis Quaid) remains lucid in other people's dreams in order to help them with their problems, which include childhood abandonment and a snakeman monster, impotence and sexual inadequacy, a fall from a skyscraper scaffold, and a crazed dream-linking assassin who wants to kill the president of the United States. Alex eventually learns the trick to staying alive while lucid dream-linking: manipulate the dream elements to his advantage.

In *The Cell*, Catherine Deame (Jennifer Lopez) encounters a different kind of challenge when she must enter the mind of a comatose serial killer, Carl Stargher (Vincent D'Onofrio). Though technically not sleeping because he cannot be awakened, Stargher nonetheless dreams because part of his brain still functions. The doctor who treats him says the killer is not just catatonic, but is in a permanent dream state until he dies. A diagnosed schizophrenic, Stargher cannot differentiate between fantasy and reality.

Once inside his sordid mind, which includes a sliced horse, a grandiose demonized version of himself, objectified women of every variety, bloody

Dream-linking therapist Catherine Deame (Jennifer Lopez) may lose her identity inside a serial killer's dream if she forgets what is real and what is an illusion in *The Cell* (New Line Cinema, 2000).

organs, and instruments of torture, Catherine may encounter the same fate. Her only chance of survival is to keep reminding herself that she is lucid dream-linking and able to manipulate dream elements to some extent (she has more control in her own dreams, according to this story). When all else fails, she can press a touch-sensitive microchip implanted in her hand.

Catherine (like Nancy in *A Nightmare on Elm Street* who brings Freddy into her reality) must bring the killer into her dreams to obtain enough power to kill him. In his dreams, she always runs the risk of losing her lucidity and/or being overpowered by his ability to manipulate his own dream.

> During a normal dream one adopts an uncritical acceptance of the events as being completely real; that is, until one either wakes up within the dream and becomes lucid, or wakes up out of sleep, at which point, in both cases, the imagery is seen as a fantasy. In dreaming we apparently lose that waking

faculty which might best be called a critical perspective. Instead, we establish a state of extreme credulity in which all self-reflective awareness appears to be suspended or dormant. The dreamer experiences a single-focused reality, and is utterly absorbed by the magic of the dream event [Godwin, 1994, 62].

Curiously, Catherine and Nancy use their lucid dreaming abilities to their best advantage while in their own dreams, while in *Dreamscape* Alex only dream-links with others. The literal and figurative monsters he encounters are always in other people's dreams, not his own. Alex's dreams are strictly off-camera.

On the other hand, in Richard Linklater's animated *Waking Life* (2001) everything on-camera is a dream. The characters within the dreams try to convince the dreamer that "dream is destiny." Constantly waking up inside of another dream, the frustrated lucid dreamer tries to distinguish reality from illusion by flicking light switches and checking the numbers on his alarm clock, as non-adjustable lighting and unreadable numbers indicate a dream state. Ultimately he discovers, however, that his lucid dream is indeed his destiny.

In *A Nightmare on Elm Street*, Nancy first hears of the idea of lucid dreaming from her boyfriend, Glen (Johnny Depp). Attempting to downplay the shared nightmares of the teenaged friends, she says, "The point is that everyone has a bad dream once in a while. It's no biggie." Glen, however, has done some reading of Balinese dream theory. He tells her, "Yeah, the next time you just tell yourself that's all it is, right while you're having it — you know, once you do that you wake right up. At least it works for me." Nancy uses his advice as a mantra to protect herself against Freddy Krueger. During the final showdown, she screams, "This is just a dream, *it* isn't real. This is just a dream, *he* isn't real." Her lucid dreaming techniques appear to destroy the fiend and turn back time to before Freddy's arrival. All seems well, until the movie's ambiguous ending leaves us with the horrifying question: Will there be a sequel?

The combination of illusion and reality takes place off-screen as well. Wes Craven, who wrote and directed *A Nightmare on Elm Street* (1984) and *Wes Craven's New Nightmare* (1994) says he got the idea for the original film from a newspaper article he read about young men with nightmares who were afraid to fall asleep.

Back in 1979, I clipped out two newspaper stories, and three years later one became *Nightmare on Elm Street* ... [The young men] would try to stay awake for a day or more, and when they finally fell asleep they would die in their sleep — apparently from suffering another, even more severe nightmare [Russo, 1992, 179].

Craven waited a year to write the script, and then waited three more years until he could find a studio willing to make the film.

Wes Craven's New Nightmare (1994) blurs the line between reality and illusion even further than its predecessors by purposely confusing the characters with the parts they play. "The implication of media in the creation of living nightmares is an important contribution to the evolution of dream sequences made by horror movies and culminates in *A Nightmare on Elm Street* (1984).... Its masking of sexual anxiety is obvious, but more significant in terms of the use of dream sequences is the implication of mass media in blurring the line between dream and reality." (Robards, 1991, 126). The fact that the *Nightmare* films have their basis in reality, i.e., lucid dreaming and the newspaper reports of the young men, make the nightmares even more threatening.

Life Is But a Dream

In films such as *Belle de Jour, Picnic at Hanging Rock, The Company of Wolves, Shattered Image,* and *Vanilla Sky,* the main characters drift in and out of dream states throughout the entire film with no set boundaries between waking and dreaming, making it difficult to draw any firm conclusions. *Picnic at Hanging Rock* begins with a voice-over warning of what will follow: "What we see, and what we seem, are but a dream. A dream within a dream." *Vanilla Sky* begins with a whispered plea: "Open your eyes. Wake up." *The Promise of Sleep* describes continuity as an important contrast between dream and reality. "Our life and events in the real world are smoothly continuous. The dream world lacks this property. Each dream tends to be an isolated event — at best, slightly related to the next" (Dement and Vaughan, 1999, 297). Abrupt shifts in time and setting, and depiction of the illogical and impossible occur in the character's lives, dreams, and dreams within dreams.

These dreamlike conditions throughout an entire film set the stage for a story that has no foundation in reality. "Some filmmakers use the medium to depict a dreamlike condition rather than a specific dream of a particular character. At such times, they employ film as a way of replicating the activities associated with the oneiric experience" (Eberwein, 1984,

Opposite: This German promotional postcard for *Wes Craven's New Nightmare* presents the crucial image for blending reality and illusion in the *Nightmare* series: Freddy Krueger's claws from a nightmare emerge from the bed into reality (New Line Cinema, 1994).

82). In these instances, our feelings about the characters' experiences may be more important than our thoughts. The only thing we safely can conclude from these films is that life is but a dream.

In films such as *All That Jazz* (1979), *Jacob's Ladder* (1990), and *Waking Life*, we also can safely conclude that death is but a dream. Godwin writes in *The Lucid Dreamer* (1994):

> One of the classic features to be found in near-death experience is that of the instantaneous life review — the drowning man who sees his life pass by in a flash. Those who have managed to return from death, or have been hypnotized into a supposed remembrance of other lives, report that every moment is played back, complete in its entirety, from the important to the most trivial [151].

Of course, we can only hear these stories from people experiencing near-death; dead men tell no tales about their dreams. In *Jacob's Ladder*, director Adrian Lyne takes viewers on a confusing surreal journey with Jacob Singer (Tim Robbins), who is a soldier in Vietnam, a happily married father of three, and a lonely postal worker with an estranged wife and a

Jacob Singer (Tim Robbins) wakes up within a dream to find himself with his girlfriend Jezzie (Elizabeth Pena) in Adrian Lyne's science fiction drama *Jacob's Ladder* (Tri-Star Pictures, 1990).

dead son now living with a woman he does not love. These three conflicting lives (of one man) flash forward and backward throughout the film as Singer dreams he is each person simultaneously. He wakes up and goes to sleep within his dreams and hallucinations. In the end, we learn the film was a flashback over his life as he lay dying on a bed in the Army field hospital.

Granted, Lyne fully intends to keep us guessing for awhile, but also provides many visual cues that indicate Singer's life is but a dream. In the life of the husband and in the life of the postal worker, he sleeps in bed and dreams, fears he is dying, displays strange symptoms, and sees irrational visions such as white-masked people trying to kill him and a nurse with a horrible growth hidden under her neat little nurse's cap. The only scenes without REM-type illogical and impossible images come during brief flashes of an attack during the war.

Despite several artistic cues in accordance with science, and the fact that Jacob's Ladder refers to Jacob from the Old Testament who experiences a dream in a field in which a ladder appears to lead him to heaven, critics were not understanding or kind to the film *Jacob's Ladder.* In *The*

Drifting in and out of consciousness from a mysterious life-threatening fever, Jacob Singer (Tim Robbins) lies in a bathtub of ice cubes in *Jacob's Ladder* (Tri-Star Pictures, 1990).

Second Century of Cinema (2000), Wheeler Winston Dixon writes of Adrian Lyne's films including *Jacob's Ladder*, saying they "constitute a litany of commercial calculation and cynical audience manipulation" (164). In *VideoHound's Golden Movie Retriever* (2001), Jim Craddock describes the film as the story of a man who becomes unable to separate reality from "the strange, psychotic world into which he increasingly lapses.... Great story potential is flawed by too many flashbacks, leaving the viewer more confused than the characters" (503). The only way to avoid confusion is to think of Singer's life and death as but a dream.

In the Old Testament, Jacob believes he has slept on holy land which inspired the dream. Upon awakening, he proceeds to strike a deal with the God revealed in his dream. "If God will be with me, and will keep me in this way that I go, and will give me bread to eat and clothing to wear, so that I come again to my father's house in peace, then the Lord shall be my God" (Genesis 28:12–21). Biblical scholar Rabbi Joseph Telushkin describes Jacob's response to the dream as incredibly bold and unlike any other in the Old Testament. "Unquestionably, Jacob's offer smacks of *chutzpah*.

Charged with a mysterious murder, stalked by an old girlfriend, and plagued with nightmares of disfigurement, David Aames (Tom Cruise) kisses his new love interest Sofia Serrano in *Vanilla Sky*. Or is he only dreaming of kissing her? (Paramount Pictures, 2001). Photograph by Neal Preston.

However, to his credit, when God does answer all of Jacob's prayers, he in turn, fulfills his side of the bargain and devotes himself loyally to God" (Telushkin, 1997, 56). The Army medics comment what a fight Singer stages to stay alive, but in the end his dreams and reality become one as he ascends a bright stairway (apparently to heaven) with his dead son.

Similarly, with its surreal blend of memories, perceptions, points of view, and self-awareness, *Vanilla Sky* is one of the most complex presentations of reality versus illusion to hit the big screen in recent years. Magazine publisher David Aames, Jr. (Tom Cruise) is trapped in a nightmare. Unaware that he is dreaming, he cannot awaken. Unaware that he is lucid dreaming, he cannot control his dreams. Unaware of what is real, he cannot distinguish illusion.

As in the case of *Jacob's Ladder*, critics were not always appreciative or receptive to these filmic dream layers that rendered the film indecipherable until the final few minutes. Critic Kirk Honeycutt writes in *The Hollywood Reporter* that the incessant interplay of dream and reality in *Vanilla Sky* leaves the audience "too fed up to give a damn where and when reality will bite" and says the film is "as pretentious as it is preposterous" and needs "its own wake-up call" (Honeycutt, 2001, 8). Certainly the concept of a dream within a dream within a dream within a dream is not for everyone. Combining death, disfigurement, cryogenics, and layers of lucid dreaming, *Vanilla Sky* portrays simultaneously conflicting story lines that defy traditional filmmaking just as dreams defy logical thought progression.

Conclusion

Returning now to the dream sequence from *In Dreams* (1998) mentioned in the Introduction, we easily can spot the technical lies that speak emotional truths. Claire Cooper (Annette Bening) falls asleep under a heavy sedative (*drugs actually reduce REM sleep, and therefore dreams*). Her eyes and body are still as she instantly makes the transition from a waking to a dreaming state (*rapid eye movement accompanies dreaming, which comes and goes throughout the night during the four stages of sleep*). We see Claire walk in slow motion through her black-and-white dream; only her bright red cape stands out from the dreary background (*slow motion usually just accompanies a nightmare in which we partially perceive our REM paralysis, and dreams, of course, are in color*). Each scene fades into another as she wanders the lonely streets (*fades and dissolves are transitional filmmaking tricks not consistent with dream logic*). A dog wails and soft music underscores the scene as she enters the abandoned Carlton Hotel filled with mysterious fog (*background music and fog are dream clichés, rather than actual dream elements*). She then approaches room 401 and enters the unlocked room to find her dead husband (Aidan Quinn) lying on the floor, his face covered with blood as a rabid dog looms over him. The dream ends abruptly, and Claire awakens remembering every detail (*we do not actually remember all the details upon awakening, but fill in the gaps as we try to piece together a story*). More importantly, she fully understands the meaning of her prophetic dream: Her husband's life is in danger from a psychopath who lives in an orchard full of red apples (*dreams are not usually straightforward, but may use symbolic language consistent with Freud's five dreamwork processes*).

Independent documentary filmmaker Alan Berliner describes dream sequences as a moviemaking trope, a cinematic metaphor "for the unpredictability of the power of the mind and the absolute synaptic speed of thought."[34] He says these shifts in time, jumps in space, and surreal leaps of logic are justified by a dream sequence because dreams operate outside conventional, literal thought structures. In addition to opening our minds to new creative connections, dreams on film also expand our emotions and help us sympathize, empathize — and sometimes criticize — because we all have first-hand experience dreaming.

When we willingly suspend disbelief for the moment and accept the filmmakers' subjective interpretations of the science of sleeping and dreaming, we also can accept the insights of these cinematic metaphors as substitutes for our own long-forgotten dreams. The degree of acceptance comes into play when filmmakers push our suspension of disbelief too far by manipulating our emotions past the point of pleasure, confusing us until we feel frustration, or brazenly violating commonly known and easily understood scientific facts about the form and content of dreams for the sake of their art.

> We want a transformation of reality that gives us insight into reality, not reality itself. The difference is really much more important than it may seem because it is the difference between reality and art. We all have reality in front of us most of the time. We have art less frequently. Realistic art is a selection of elements which conveys the illusion of reality [Martin and Jacobus, 416].

Although science contains its own beauty in the facts of literal truth, art possesses the beauty of emotions in figurative truth.

In the wake, so to speak, of scientific advancements in areas such as REM sleep, lucid dreaming, and sleep disorders, people still crave the familiar stuff that Freud's dreams are made of — aggression, violence, and sexual symbols. The general public, movie-goers, and filmmakers still embrace Freud's theory of dreams as repressed wishes, an eternal, universal condition to which we can all relate. John Beebe writes in his essay "Jungian Illumination of Film" that "cinema has grown up concurrently with psychoanalysis, and as close siblings nurtured on a common zeitgeist, the two share a drive to explore and realize the psyche" (579). This mysterious power of the unconscious mind revealed in dream sequences has struck a personal chord among audiences since the earliest films around 1900 when the cinematic struggle between art and science began.

Freud says a dream within a dream is the core, that the most abstracted level of a dream within the dream is the reality. Writer-director M. Night Shyamalan has the right idea in *The Sixth Sense* (1999). The aptly named Cole Sear (Haley Joel Osment), a boy who is blessed/cursed with a sixth sense of seeing dead people, says to child psychologist Malcolm Crowe (Bruce Willis): "I got an idea how you can talk to your wife. Wait till she's asleep, then she'll listen to you and she won't even know it."

Indeed the altered state of consciousness associated with sleeping and dreaming makes us more receptive to new ideas, especially when they concern our two basic instincts of sex and death. The dreamlike state of watching a film can be used as a means of getting people to listen to ideas they might otherwise ignore (a trick utilized within *Stir of Echoes* [1999]). Therefore, a dream within this dream, i.e., a filmed dream sequence, should have even more impact.

In this cinematic struggle between art and science, audiences will forego the literal truth of sleeping and dreaming if the emotional truth of the dream within a dream is valid and the dream sequence does not veer too far from the realm of possibility. Watching dreams on film that effectively combine the literal and the figurative, the intellectual and the emotional, the scientific and the artistic is never a struggle for the viewer, however. In the hands of the right director, the combination leaves us spellbound.

Filmography

Information on films cited in this work is included below. These films are representative of various waking, sleeping, and dreaming states as depicted in movies from the mid-twentieth century through 2002 and are not intended as a comprehensive listing of all dreams on film. Films titles are followed by the director, year released, two lead actors, and a description of the film as it relates to the subject of dreams on film.

Akira Kurosawa's Dreams (Akira Kurosawa, 1990) Akira Terao, Mitsuko Baisho
Acclaimed Japanese director explores nature, myth, death, and humanity through thematically linked short films based on his actual dreams.

All That Jazz (Bob Fosse, 1979) Roy Scheider, Jessica Lange
Part dream, part flashback, a chain-smoking choreographer-director reviews his life while dying in a hospital bed.

All the Pretty Horses (Billy Bob Thornton, 2000) Matt Damon, Penelope Cruz
A Texas cowboy moves to Mexico and has wish fulfillment dreams of pretty horses and a pretty woman.

Altered States (Ken Russell, 1980) William Hurt, Blair Brown
An obsessive college professor experiments with hallucinogenic mushrooms, isolation tanks, and altered states of consciousness in order to explore Jung's concept of the collective unconscious.

American Beauty (Sam Mendes, 1999) Kevin Spacey, Annette Bening
A middle-aged man escapes his dreary existence by daydreaming about his teenage daughter's sexy classmate.

Analyze This (Harold Ramis, 1998) Billy Crystal, Robert De Niro
A tough mobster endures a mid-life crisis with accompanying panic attacks, crying spells, and Oedipal dreams.

Another Woman (Woody Allen, 1988) Gena Rowlands, Gene Hackman
An emotionally dead middle-aged woman has troubling dreams, daydreams, and flashbacks of her cold-hearted past.

Awakenings (Penny Marshall, 1990) Robin Williams, Robert De Niro
The true story about catatonic patients "awakening" with use of the drug L-dopa.

Babe (Chris Noonan, 1995) James Cromwell, Magna Szubanski
One highly intelligent pig is depicted in altered states of consciousness as he learns the art of sheep herding.

Being John Malkovich (Spike Jonze, 1999) John Cusack, Cameron Diaz
A supernatural portal takes people into the consciousness of actor John Malkovich for fifteen minutes before dumping them onto a highway.

Belle de Jour (Luis Bunuel, 1967) Catherine Deneuve, Jean Sorel
A frigid newlywed has masochistic dreams and daydreams about life as a prostitute in a film that effectively blends reality and illusion.

The Blair Witch Project (Eduardo Sanchez/Daniel Myrick, 1999) Heather Donahue, Michael Williams
Three novice filmmakers are deprived of sleep, food, and safety as they hunt for a witch in the woods in this pseudo documentary.

Bram Stoker's Dracula (Francis Ford Coppola, 1992) Gary Oldman, Winona Ryder
Count Dracula feasts on his victims as they sleep.

The Burkittsville 7 (Ben Rock, 2000) John Maynard, Lucy Butler
A pseudo documentary about child murders that jumps back and forth through time, using memories, film footage, still photography and interviews to present the evolution of crime and punishment.

Cat People (Paul Schrader, 1982) Nastassja Kinski, Malcolm McDowell
A young woman who learns of her bizarre genetic heritage dreams of returning to her feline friends.

The Cell (Tarsem Singh, 2000) Jennifer Lopez, Vince Vaughn
A kind-hearted female psychotherapist must enter the consciousness of a comatose serial killer and heal his inner child in order to save a woman's life.

City Edition (Alan Berliner, 1980)
This experimental short film uses black and white found footage to take us inside a man's dream as he processes the daily news.

Coming to America (John Landis, 1988) Eddie Murphy, Arsenio Hall
Prince Akeem of Zamunda awakens on his twenty-first birthday eager to break tradition and choose his own bride.

The Company of Wolves (Neil Jordan, 1984) Angela Lansbury, David Warner
An adolescent girl dreams of losing her virginity to the Big Bad Wolf.

Cries and Whispers (Ingmar Bergman, 1972) Harriet Andersson, Ingrid Thulin
Three repressed sisters and their servant have dreams, fantasies, and flashbacks as one sister lies dying.

Dark City (Alex Proyas, 1997) Kiefer Sutherland, Rufus Sewell
Sinister aliens take over the minds of sleeping earthlings.

Despair (R.W. Fassbinder, 1977) Dirk Bogarde, Andrea Ferreol

A disturbed chocolate factory owner hallucinates and dreams his way into destruction and death.

Dreamscape (Joseph Ruben, 1984) Dennis Quaid, Kate Capshaw
An underachieving psychic discovers his heroic qualities through dream-linking experiments at a sleep lab.

Dudley Do-Right (Hugh Wilson, 1999) Brendan Fraser, Alfred Molina
Dim-witted Canadian Mountie Dudley Do-Right dreams of finding his lost horse and exposing a gold rush scam devised by his nemesis, Snidely Whiplash.

Dumb and Dumber (Peter Farrelly, 1994) Jim Carrey, Jeff Daniels
Two moronic friends go on a road trip and daydream along the way.

8½ (Federico Fellini, 1963) Marcello Mastroianni, Claudia Cardinale
Fellini's self-portrait about an Italian film director re-evaluating his life and career through dreams, flashbacks, and fantasies.

End of Days (Peter Hyams, 1999) Arnold Schwarzenegger, Gabriel Byrne
A 21-year-old woman has recurrent dreams of having sex with the devil.

Fiddler on the Roof (Norman Jewison, 1971) Chaim Topol, Norma Crane
A poor Jewish dairy farmer fakes a prophetic dream about his daughter's marriage in order to persuade his wife that the wedding is a mistake.

Field of Dreams (Phil Alden Robinson, 1989) Kevin Costner, Amy Madigan
An Iowa farmer builds a baseball diamond in a corn field and shares a telepathic dream with his wife about its significance.

Final Analysis (Phil Joanou, 1992) Richard Gere, Uma Thurman
A gullible psychiatrist is tricked by a patient's use of a sexually symbolic dream from Freud's *The Interpretation of Dreams*.

Fletch (Michael Ritchie, 1985) Chevy Chase, Tim Matheson
A wise-cracking investigative reporter hunted by police, targeted for murder, and on the brink of being fired dreams he is a famous basketball player.

Frightened to Death (Christian J. Otjen, 1987) Gilbert Shine, Christian J. Otjen
An aging stage director, his beautiful young wife, and the stage manager make a dangerous, nightmare-inducing love triangle.

Goldfinger (Guy Hamilton, 1964) Sean Connery, Honor Blackman
James Bond, Agent 007, meets the woman of his erotic dreams, Pussy Galore, and the man of his nightmares, her evil gold-smuggling employer, Goldfinger.

Gordy (Mark Lewis, 1995) Michael Roescher, Kristy Young
A talking pig, shown in altered states of consciousness, enlists the help of two children to save his family.

Groundhog Day (Harold Ramis, 1993) Bill Murray, Andie MacDowell
A TV weatherman with a bad attitude gets stuck in a time loop and must wake to the same day each morning until he gets it right.

Hollow Man (Paul Verhoeven, 2000) Kevin Bacon, Elisabeth Shue
A woman scientist dreams of her former boyfriend, now a psychotic invisible genius who rapes her as she sleeps.

In Dreams (Neil Jordan, 1998) Annette Bening, Robert Downey, Jr.
A woman is psychically linked to a serial killer through her dreams.

Insomnia (Christopher Nolan, 2002) Al Pacino, Robin Williams
A Los Angeles cop with a guilty conscience has trouble sleeping while he hunts a killer in Alaska.

Into the Night (John Landis, 1985) Jeff Goldblum, Michelle Pfeiffer
A bored aerospace engineer finds an unusual cure for his insomnia by giving a ride to a beautiful jewel smuggler.

Jacob's Ladder (Adrian Lyne, 1990) Tim Robbins, Elizabeth Pena
Through a series of flashbacks and dreams (all within an overall dream), a soldier reviews his life and loves.

Jump Tomorrow (Joel Hopkins, 2000) Tunde Adebimpe, Hippolyte Girardot
An introverted man dreams and daydreams about himself as a confident star in a Spanish soap opera.

Jurassic Park III (Joe Johnston, 2001) Sam Neill, Tea Leoni
An ill-fated paleontologist dreams of a talking velociraptor while onboard an airplane.

Keeping the Faith (Edward Norton, 2000) Edward Norton, Ben Stiller
A priest has erotic dreams about a woman he has known since childhood.

Kindergarten Cop (Ivan Reitman, 1990) Arnold Schwarzenegger, Penelope Ann Miller
A muscular cop working undercover as a kindergarten teacher falls asleep at his desk and dreams of the vicious criminal he is working to arrest.

Lady in the Box (Christian J. Otjen, 2000) Darren E. Burrows, Robert Knepper
A naive young man makes noises in his girlfriend's ear while she sleeps in order to induce nightmares, which she relates upon awakening.

Lara Croft: Tomb Raider (Simon West, 2001) Angelina Jolie, Noah Taylor
A thrill-loving heiress dreams of her missing father and the archeological secrets he took with him.

The Last Temptation of Christ (Martin Scorsese, 1988) Willem Dafoe, Harvey Keitel
While nailed to the cross, Christ experiences a prophetic dream that serves as his last earthly temptation.

Living in Oblivion (Tom DiCillo, 1994) Steve Buscemi, Catherine Keener
A director and actress dream about their low-budget independent film, which includes a smokey dream sequence with a cranky dwarf.

Marnie (Alfred Hitchcock, 1964) Tippi Hedren, Sean Connery
Beautiful man-hating kleptomaniac Marnie has recurring dreams about her troubled past.

The Mask (Chuck Russell, 1994) Jim Carrey, Cameron Diaz
Stanley, a nerdy bank clerk, finds a supernatural mask that releases his alter ego and prompts a dream of a wild night at the hottest club in town.

The Matrix (Andy and Larry Wachowski, 1999) Keanu Reeves, Carrie-Anne Moss
A handsome young computer hacker risks his life to wake up the world from its computer-generated dream.

Men in Black (Barry Sonnenfeld, 1997) Will Smith, Tommy Lee Jones
Sharply dressed top secret government operatives rearrange their sleeping schedules to investigate alien activities on earth.

The Mummy Returns (Stephen Sommers, 2001) Brendan Fraser, Rachel Weisz
An adventurer and his wife explore an ancient temple where she experiences visions and feelings of déjà vu.

National Lampoon's European Vacation (Amy Heckerling, 1985) Chevy Chase, Beverly D'Angelo
The hapless Griswold family travels to Europe and enjoys wish fulfillment dreams en route.

National Lampoon's Vacation (Harold Ramis, 1983) Chevy Chase, Beverly D'Angelo
The Griswold family survives a disastrous cross-country road trip despite an episode where Clark Griswold falls asleep while driving.

A Nightmare on Elm Street (Wes Craven, 1984) Heather Langenkamp, Robert Englund
Four teens share the same nightmare about a disfigured child killer named Freddy Krueger.

A Nightmare on Elm Street 2: Freddy's Revenge (Jack Sholder, 1985) Mark Patton, Robert Englund
More teenagers are stalked in their sleep through high-tech dream sequences.

A Nightmare on Elm Street 3: Dream Warriors (Chuck Russell, 1987) Patricia Arquette, Robert Englund
The heroine from the first *Nightmare* film returns to counsel the latest victim of nightmares invaded by psychopathic Freddy.

A Nightmare on Elm Street 4: Dream Master (Renny Harlin, 1988) Rodney Eastman, Robert Englund
A telepathic girl proves a challenge for a dream-invading child killer.

A Nightmare on Elm Street 5: The Dream Child (Stephen Hopkins, 1989) Lisa Wilcox, Robert Englund
The nightmare continues as Freddy haunts the dreams of an unborn fetus.

Ordinary People (Robert Redford, 1980) Mary Tyler Moore, Timothy Hutton
A troubled young man has nightmares reliving a childhood boating accident in which his brother was killed.

Panic (Henry Bromell, 2000) William H. Macy, Donald Sutherland
A middle-aged hitman reconsiders his life of crime through a series of flashbacks.

Paperhouse (Bernard Rose, 1989) Glenne Headly, Ben Cross
A lonely young girl's recurring dreams intrude upon her waking life.

Papillon (Franklin J. Schaffner, 1973) Steve McQueen, Dustin Hoffman

An innocent man convicted of murdering a pimp is sent to a brutal French prison where he dreams during solitary confinement.

Pee-wee's Big Adventure (Tim Burton, 1985) Paul Reubens, Elizabeth (E.G.) Daily
When Pee-wee's beloved bike is stolen, he has recurrent anxiety dreams.

Persona (Ingmar Bergman, 1966) Bibi Andersson, Liv Ullmann
Through dreams and hallucinations, a young nurse and her manipulative patient blend identities.

Phantasm II (Don A. Coscarelli, 1988) James LeGros, Reggie Bannister
Two psychic teens share dreams about a deadly Tall Man.

Picnic at Hanging Rock (Peter Weir, 1975) Margaret Nelson, Rachel Roberts
Presented simultaneously as a factual account and as an adolescent's dream of wish fulfillment, a girls' school picnic turns into tragedy.

The Princess Bride (Rob Reiner, 1987) Cary Elwes, Robin Wright
Beautiful Buttercup has an anxiety dream about becoming a princess.

Raising Arizona (Joel Coen, 1987) Nicolas Cage, Holly Hunter
A small-time criminal sees his future in a dream.

Risky Business (Paul Brickman, 1983) Tom Cruise, Rebecca DeMornay
A teenager has sexy wish fulfillment dreams.

Rosemary's Baby (Roman Polanski, 1968) Mia Farrow, John Cassavetes
An innocent young woman dreams that she has been impregnated by the devil.

See Spot Run (John Whitesell, 2001) David Arquette, Michael Clarke Duncan
A dog-hating postal carrier finds a dog who endures painful flashbacks to its days as a puppy training for the FBI.

The Sender (Roger Christian, 1982) Kathryn Harrod, Zeljko Ivanek
A suicidal amnesiac young man sends nightmares to others when he sleeps.

Shattered Image (Raul Ruiz, 1998) Anne Parillaud, William Baldwin
A woman on her honeymoon dreams she is an assassin or is she an assassin dreaming she is a woman on her honeymoon?

The Sixth Sense (M. Night Shyamalan, 1999) Bruce Willis, Haley Joel Osment
A therapist in a troubled marriage treats a strange boy with nightmares and visions who helps him better communicate with his wife.

Sleeper (Woody Allen, 1973) Woody Allen, Diane Keaton
A nerd wakes up in a sexless society after sleeping for two hundred years.

Sleeping Beauty (Clyde Geronimi, 1959) Mary Costa, Bill Shirley
The animated princess sleepwalks, then falls into a deathlike sleep for one hundred years.

Sleepless in Seattle (Nora Ephron, 1993) Tom Hanks, Meg Ryan
A widowed man and his son share sleepless nights and troubled dreams.

Sleepy Hollow (Tim Burton, 1999) Johnny Depp, Christina Ricci
A man of science sent to solve supernatural murders, Ichabod Crane dreams of his mother's persecution for witchcraft.

Snow Dogs (Brian Levant, 2002) Cuba Gooding, Jr., James Coburn
A man's painful experience of learning about his true heritage is lightened by humorous dreams about his infancy and a pack of talking dogs.

Snow White and the Seven Dwarfs (David Hand, 1937) Adriana Caselotti, Harry Stockwell
The animated adaptation of a young girl, her jealous stepmother, and a noxious sleeping potion.

Spellbound (Alfred Hitchcock, 1945) Gregory Peck, Ingrid Bergman
An amnesiac regains his identity through a psychiatrist's interpretation of his dream.

Star Wars: Episode II — Attacks of the Clones (George Lucas, 2002) Natalie Portman, Hayden Christensen
A young Jedi apprentice has recurrent nightmares about his mother.

Stigmata (Rupert Wainwright, 1999) Patricia Arquette, Gabriel Byrne
A young hairstylist endures terrifying religious visions brought on by stolen rosary beads from a dead priest.

Stir of Echoes (David Koepp, 1999) Kevin Bacon, Illeana Douglas
An ordinary guy develops the ability to see the future through visions, dreams, and hallucinations.

The Story of Adele H. (Francois Truffaut, 1975) Isabelle Adjani, Bruce Robinson
A young woman suffers from recurrent nightmares about her sister's death by drowning.

Stranger (Scott Crowell, 2000) Scott Crowell, Scott Walters
A dangerous stranger hitchhikes through the country in an altered state of consciousness.

The Talented Mr. Ripley (Anthony Minghella, 1999) Matt Damon, Jude Law
A psychotic young man's guilty conscience produces troubling nightmares.

The Terminator (James Cameron, 1984) Arnold Schwarzenegger, Linda Hamilton
A hero from the future dreams of his youth on post-nuclear earth run by ruthless cyborg killing machines.

Terminator 2: Judgment Day (James Cameron, 1991) Arnold Schwarzenegger, Linda Hamilton
Hunted by a T-1000, the deadliest terminator of them all, Sarah Conner has a prophetic dream about a nuclear holocaust.

The Time Machine (Simon Wells, 2002) Guy Pearce, Jeremy Irons
A grieving inventor creates a time machine that takes him into a future where an underground monster telepathically transmits nightmares to above-ground dwellers.

Total Recall (Paul Verhoeven, 1990) Arnold Schwarzenegger, Rachel Ticotin
A construction worker has recurrent dreams about the planet Mars and a sleazy, dark-haired, athletic woman.

Twelve Monkeys (Terry Gilliam, 1995) Bruce Willis, Madeleine Stowe

Troubled by recurring dreams, a prisoner from the future is sent back to the 1990s to investigate the origins of a deadly plague.

Vanilla Sky (Cameron Crowe, 2001) Tom Cruise, Penelope Cruz
A disfigured publisher cannot tell the difference between dreams and reality.

Vertigo (Alfred Hitchcock, 1958) James Stewart, Kim Novak
A retired detective with vertigo dreams of falling from heights and falling in love.

Waking Life (Richard Linklater, 2001) Wiley Wiggins, Ethan Hawke
A young man cannot awaken from his dream in this animated exploration of consciousness.

Warlock 3: The End of Innocence (Eric Freiser, 1998) Bruce Payne, Ashley Laurence
An inherited mansion links a young woman to an evil warlock who appears in her dreams.

Wes Craven's New Nightmare (Wes Craven, 1994) Heather Langenkamp, Robert Englund
A spooky spoof of the *"Nightmare"* series in which Freddy Krueger haunts the dreams of the actress who battled him in earlier movies, possesses her young son, and kills her husband.

Wild Strawberries (Ingmar Bergman, 1957) Victor Sjostrom, Bibi Andersson
An elderly professor has disturbing dreams about his youth.

William Shakespeare's A Midsummer Night's Dream (Michael Hoffman, 1999) Kevin Kline, Michelle Pfeiffer
Humans and fairies confuse their dream life with reality in turn-of-the-century Tuscany.

Willy Wonka & the Chocolate Factory (Mel Stuart, 1971) Gene Wilder, Jack Albertson
An eccentric candyman makes literal and figurative dreams come true.

With a Friend Like Harry (Dominik Moll, 2000) Laurent Lucas, Sergi Lopez
A psychotic former high school classmate induces strange dreams of propeller-headed monkeys in the mind of an ordinary family man.

The Wizard of Oz (Victor Fleming, 1939) Judy Garland, Margaret Hamilton
A Kansas farm girl displaces her feelings about people into colorful dreams.

Notes

Part I

1. Film quotations are taken directly from spoken dialogue or subtitles of American prints of the films.
2. Byrne, Gabriel. Interview with author. Maitland, Florida, June 17, 2001.
3. Crowell, Scott. Telephone interview with author. November 30, 2000.
4. Rock, Ben. Interview with author. Winter Park, Florida, October 29, 2000.
5. Berliner, Alan. Personal correspondence with author. July 7, 2001.
6. *Ibid.*
7. Rock, Ben. Interview with author. Winter Park, Florida, October 29, 2000.
8. Berliner, Alan. Personal correspondence with author. July 7, 2001.
9. *Ibid.*

Part II

10. Bromell, Henry. Telephone interview with author. September 18, 2000.
11. *Ibid.*
12. Crowell, Scott. Telephone interview with author. November 30, 2000.
13. All biblical references come from the *Holy Bible.* Revised Standard Version. Nashville: Thomas Nelson, Inc., Old Testament Section 1952, New Testament Section 1971.
14. Byrne, Gabriel. Interview with author. Maitland, Florida, June 17, 2001.
15. No Strings Attached 'N Sync World Tour 2000. Produced and directed by Marty Callner for HBO. A Cream Cheese Films Production, 2000.
16. McGee, Celia. From a syndicated story in *The Orlando Sentinel* (January 15, 2001, A2); originally published in (New York) *Daily News.*
17. Byrne, Gabriel. Interview with author. Maitland, Florida, June 17, 2001.
18. Compiled from staff and wire reports. "Satan as a Real Being," News to Note in *The Orlando Sentinel* (Saturday, July 7, 2001, E-6).
19. Cox News Service. From a syndicated story in *The Orlando Sentinel* (July 9, 2000, A-12).
20. Rock, Ben. Interview with author. Winter Park, Florida, October 29, 2000.

21. Crowell, Scott. Telephone interview with author. November 30, 2000.

22. Rock, Ben. Interview with author. Winter Park, Florida, October 29, 2000.

23. *Ibid.*

24. Byrne, Gabriel. Interview with author. Maitland, Florida, June 17, 2001.

25. Hopkins, Joel. Interview with author. Maitland, Florida, June 14, 2001.

26. Adebimpe, Tunde. Interview with author. Maitland, Florida, June 14, 2001.

27. Hopkins, Joel. Interview with author. Maitland, Florida, June 14, 2001.

28. Otjen, Christian J. Telephone interview with author. October 23, 2000.

29. Otjen, Christian J. Personal correspondence with author. July 2, 2001.

30. Bromell, Henry. Telephone interview with author. September 18, 2000.

31. Rock, Ben. Interview with author. Winter Park, Florida, October 29, 2000.

32. *Ibid.*

33. *Ibid.*

34. Berliner, Alan. Personal correspondence with author. July 7, 2001.

Bibliography

Anderson, Mary. *Colour Therapy*. Great Britain: William Collins, 1990.

Andrews, Sam. "THR E-mail: In Dreams." *The Hollywood Reporter* (October 2, 2000).

Antrobus, John S., and Howard Ehrlichman. "The Dream Report: Attention, Memory, Functional Hemispheric Asymmetry, and Memory Organization." In *Sleep, Dreams and Memory*, ed. William Fishbein. New York: Spectrum Publications, 1981; page 137.

Beebe, John. "Jungian Illumination of Film." *National Psychological Association for Psychoanalysis*. Vol. 83, (August 1996).

Berman, Emanuel. "The Film Viewer: From Dreamer to Dream Interpreter." *Psychoanalytic Inquiry*. Vol. 18, No. 2, (1998).

Braudy, Leo. *The World in a Frame*. New York: Anchor Books, 1977.

Bulkeley, Kelly. "Touring the Dream Factory: The Dream-Film Connection in *The Wizard of Oz* and *A Nightmare on Elm Street*." *Dreaming: Journal of the Association for the Study of Dreams*. Vol. 9, No. 1. (November 1999).

Cohen, Marc, S., Patricia Curd, and C.D.C. Reeve. Ed. *Readings in Ancient Greek Philosophy*. Indianapolis: Hackett Publishing Company, 1995.

Condon, Paul, and Jim Sangster. *The Complete Hitchcock*. London: Virgin Publishing Ltd., 1999.

Conklin, Mike. "Terrorist attacks have become national nightmare." *The Orlando Sentinel*. (October, 3, 2001).

Conrad, Joseph. *Heart of Darkness*. London: England: Penguin Group, 1995.

Craddock, Jim, ed. *VideoHound's Golden Movie Retriever 2001*. Farmington Hills, Mich.: Visible Ink Press, 2001.

The Dalai Lama and J. Varela Francisco, Ph.D., editor and narrator. *Sleeping, Dreaming, and Dying*. Boston: Wisdom Publications, 1997.

Darwin, Charles. *The Origin of Species*. New York: Literary Classics.

Dee, Nerys. *Understanding and Interpreting Dreams*. New York: Sterling, 1990.

_____. *Your Dreams and What They Mean*. New York: Bell, 1984.

Dement, William C. and Christopher Vaughan. *The Promise of Sleep*. New York: Random House, 1999.

Dixon, Wheeler Winston. *The Second Century of Cinema*. Albany, N.Y.: State University of New York Press, 2000.

Eastman, John. *Retakes. Behind the Scenes of 500 Classic Movies*. New York: Ballantine, 1989.

Ebert, Roger. *Roger Ebert's Movie Home Companion*. Kansas City, Mo.: Andrews, McMeel & Parker, 1986.

Eberwein, Robert T. *Film and the Dream Screen: A Sleep and a Forgetting*. Princeton, N.J.: Princeton University Press, 1984.

Esslin, Martin. *The Age of Television*. New York: W.H. Freeman, 1982.

Fishbein, William, ed. *Sleep, Dreams and Memory*. New York: Spectrum, 1981.

Fisher, Charles, et al. "The Nightmare." In *Sleep and Dreaming*, edited by Ernest Hartmann. Boston: Little, Brown, 1970.

Flanagan, Owen. *Dreaming Souls: Sleep, Dreams, and the Evolution of the Conscious Mind*. New York: Oxford University Press, 2000.

Freud, Sigmund. *Civilization and Its Discontents*, translated by James Strachey. New York: W.W. Norton, 1961.

_____. *The Freud Reader*, edited by Peter Gay. New York: W.W. Norton, 1989.

_____. *The Interpretation of Dreams*, translated by A.A. Brill. New York: Modern Library, 1994.

Gabbard, Glen O. "The Psychoanalyst at the Movies." *The International Journal of Psycho-analysis*. Vol: 78, (June 1997).

Gamwell, Lynn, ed. *Dreams 1900–2000: Science, Art and the Unconscious Mind*. New York: Cornell University Press, 2000.

Gell-Mann, Murray. *The Quark and the Jaguar: Adventures in the Simple and the Complex*. New York: W.H. Freeman, 1994.

Giannetti, Louis D. *Understanding Movies*. Englewood Cliffs, N.J.: Prentice-Hall, 1972.

Godwin, Malcolm. *The Lucid Dreamer*. New York: Labyrinth, 1994.

Goode, Erica. "Rats May Dream, It Seems, of Their Days at the Mazes." *The New York Times* (January 25, 2001).

Gottlieb, Sidney, ed. *Hitchcock on Hitchcock: Selected Writings and Interviews*. Berkeley: University of California Press, 1995.

Hall, Calvin S. and Vernon J. Nordby. *A Primer of Jungian Psychology*. New York: New American Library, 1973.

Halpern, Leslie. "Dracula Had Bloodletting, Coppola Says." *The Hollywood Reporter* (September 9, 1992).

_____. "Dreams, Opium, and the Creation of Kubla Khan." *The Journal of Graduate Liberal Studies*. Vol. VII, No. 1, (Fall, 2001).

_____. "Panic." *Markee Magazine*. Vol. 15, No. 12 (December 2000).

_____. "Scaring Up Hype." *The Orlando Sentinel* (February 16, 1999).

_____. "Stranger." *Markee Magazine*. Vol. 16, No. 2 (February 2001).

Haltof, Marek. "A Dream Within a Dream." *S. European Journal for Semiotic Studies*. Vol. 2, No. 1 (1990).

Hamilton, Edith. *Mythology*. New York: Little, Brown, 1969.

Hartmann, Ernest. "The Functions of Sleep and Memory Processing." In *Sleep, Dreams and Memory*, edited by William Fishbein. New York: Spectrum, 1981.

_____. "The Psychology and Physiology of Dreaming." In *Dreams 1900–2000: Science, Art and the Unconscious Mind*, edited by Lynn Gamwell. New York: Cornell University Press, 2000.

_____. ed., *Sleep and Dreaming*. Boston: Little, Brown, 1970.

Honeycutt, Kirk. "Vanilla Sky." *The Hollywood Reporter*. (Monday, December 10, 2001).

Jones, Richard. "Possible Functions of Dreaming." *Sleep and Dreaming*. Edited by Ernest Hartmann. Boston: Little, Brown and Company, Inc., 1970.

Jung, C.G. *Dreams*. Translated by R.F.C. Hull. Princeton, New Jersey: Princeton University Press, 1974.

_____. *Memories, Dreams, Reflections*, recorded and edited by Aniela Jaffe, translated by Richard and Clara Winston. New York: Vintage Books, 1989.

_____. *Modern Man in Search of a Soul*, translated by W.S. Dell and Cary F. Baynes. New York: Harcourt Brace, 1933.

_____. *Psychology and Religion*. New Haven: Yale University Press, 1938.

_____. *The Spirit in Man, Art, and Literature*, translated by R.F.C. Hull. Princeton, N.J.: Princeton University Press, 1966.

Koch-Sheras, Phyllis, and Amy Lemley. *The Dream Sourcebook*. Los Angeles: RGA Publishing Group, 1995.

Lewis, James R. *The Dream Encyclopedia*. Detroit, Mich.: Visible Ink Press, 1995.

Loukides, Paul, and Linda K. Fuller, Ed. *Beyond the Stars II: Plot Conventions in American Popular Film*. Bowling Green, Ohio: Bowling Green State University Popular Press, 1991.

Madow, Leo, and Laurence H. Snow. Ed. *The Psychodynamic Implications of the Physiological Studies on Dreams*. Springfield, Ill.: Charles C. Thomas, 1970.

Martin, F. David, and Lee A. Jacobus. *Humanities Through the Arts*. New York: McGraw-Hill, 1975.

Maxfield, James F. "Dreaming With Bergman." *The Willamette Journal of the Liberal Arts*. Vol. 4, No. 1 (Winter 1998–1999).

Mazza, Joan. *Dreaming Your Real Self*. New York: Berkley, 1998.

McCarthy, Cormac. *All the Pretty Horses*. New York: Vintage Books, 1992.

McDonnell, David, Ed. *Starlog's Science Fiction Heroes and Heroines*. New York: Crescent Books, 1995.

Melbourne, David F., and Keith Hearne. *Dream Interpretation: The Secret*. London: Blandford, 1997.

Miles, Jack. *GOD: A Biography*. New York: Vintage Books, 1995.

Miller, Gustavus Hindman. *A Dictionary of Dreams*. New York: Smithmark Publishers, 1992.

Morgan, Lucien. *Dreams and Symbols*. New York: Smithmark Publishers, 1996.

Moss, Robert. *Dreamgates*. New York: Three Rivers Press, 1998.

Naughton, John, and Adam Smith. *Movies: A Crash Course*. New York: Watson-Guptill, 1998.

Pascal, Blaise. *Selections from the Thoughts*, edited and translated by Arthur H. Beattie. Illinois: Harlan Davidson, 1965.

Pearlman, Chester A. "The Adaptive Function of Dreaming." *Sleep and Dreaming*, edited by Ernest Hartmann. Boston: Little, Brown, 1970.

Perkins, David, ed. *English Romantic Writers*. Fort Worth, Tex.: Harcourt Brace, 1995.

Restak, Richard M. *The Mind*. New York: Bantam Books, 1988.

Robards, Brooks. "California Dreaming: Dream Sequences in Hollywood Musicals, Melodramas and Horror Movies." In *Beyond the Stars II: Plot Conventions in American Popular Film*, edited by Paul Loukides and Linda K. Fuller. Bowling Green, Ohio: Bowling Green State University Popular Press, 1991.

Russo, John. *Scare Tactics*. New York: Dell, 1992.

Rzepka, Charles J., *The Self as Mind*. Cambridge, Mass.: Harvard University Press, 1986.

Saint Augustine. *The Confessions of St. Augustine*, translated by Rex Warner. New York: Penguin Books, 1963.

Sarna, Nahum M. *The JPS Torah Commentary: Genesis*. New York: Jewish Publication Society, 1989.

Sarris, Andrew. *The American Cinema*. New York: E.P. Dutton, 1968.

Schoenewolf, Gerald. *The Dictionary of Dream Interpretation*. Northvale, N.J.: Jason Aronson, Inc., 1997.

Schwartz, Wynn. "Problem Representation in Dreams." In *The Kekule Riddle: A Challenge for Chemists and Psychologists*, edited by John H. Wotiz. Carbondale, Ill.: Glendale Press, 1993.

Spitz, Ellen Handler. "Film as Dream." *Image and Insight: Essays in Psychoanalysis and the Arts*. New York: Columbia University Press, 1991.

Telushkin, Rabbi Joseph. *Biblical Literacy*. New York: William Morrow, 1997.

Thompson, Frank. "Dream Logic." *American Film*. Vol. 15 (March 1990).

Van De Castle, Robert L. *Our Dreaming Mind*. New York: Ballantine, 1994.

Wilson, Edward O. *Consilience: The Unity of Knowledge*. New York: Alfred A. Knopf, 1998.

Wood, Michael. "Double Lives." *Sight and Sound*. Vol. 1, No. 9 (January 1992).

Zucker, Carole. "Sweetest Tongue Has Sharpest Tooth: The Dangers of Dreaming in Neil Jordan's *The Company of Wolves*." *Literature/Film Quarterly*. Vol. 28, No. 1 (2000).

Index